Voice Speech for Musical Theatre

About the Author

Chris Palmer, BA PGDIP, SFHEA, is a pioneer in the integration of voice and singing specializing in musical theatre. For over five years, she was a vocal coach on *Mamma Mia*. She has trained countless performers as Head of Voice at Guildford School of Acting over the last fourteen years, many of whom now have leading roles across almost every show in the West End. Chris also trains politicians both nationally and internationally (including formerly at the World Economic Forum in Geneva), PhD students and lawyers, and provides voice training for staff at the University of Surrey on vocal delivery and maximizing their vocal potential.

Voice and Speech for Musical Theatre

A Practical Guide

Chris Palmer

methuen | drama

LONDON • NEW YORK • OXFORD • NEW DELHI • SYDNEY

METHUEN DRAMA
Bloomsbury Publishing Plc
50 Bedford Square, London, WC1B 3DP, UK
1385 Broadway, New York, NY 10018, USA

BLOOMSBURY, METHUEN DRAMA and the Methuen Drama logo are
trademarks of Bloomsbury Publishing Plc

First published in Great Britain 2020
Reprinted 2020

A catalogue record for this book is available from the British Library.

A catalog record for this book is available from the Library of Congress.

ISBN: HB: 978-1-3500-1124-3
      PB: 978-1-3500-1125-0
      ePDF: 978-1-3500-1123-6
      eBook: 978-1-3500-1126-7

Series: Performance Books

Typeset by RefineCatch Limited, Bungay, Suffolk
Printed and bound in Great Britain

To find out more about our authors and books visit www.bloomsbury.com
and sign up for our newsletters.

In honour of Stephen Clark (lyricist and playwright) who gave me the confidence to write it all down, and Ian Palmer my baby brother, who knew when it was time to lay down.

Contents

List of Figures ix
Foreword I *Ian Talbot* x
Foreword II *Michael Jibson* xii
Preface for Teachers xiii
Preface for Students xvii
Acknowledgements xx

Introduction 1
   An overview 4
   My philosophy 5
   Video 7
   Further reading 7

1   Posture, Alignment and Neutral Plus 9
   Introduction 9
   Neutral plus (N+): The foundations, feet first and the body 15
   The postural changes: For speech, song and dance 35
   Further reading 42

2   Breath, Dance and Movement 43
   Introduction 43
   Breath management and stamina 44
   Gym breath into speech and song 63
   Dance, voice and movement 66
   Further reading 76

3   Building the Voice 77

Introduction 77
Vowels 78
Placement of sound 82
Building the vocal set using animals, archetypes, myths
and legends 86
Intoning the sound 89
Vowels and their modification, in and out of fashion 97
Further reading 103

4   Pitch and Tune 105

Introduction 105
High and low: Playing with pitch 108
Building the pitch 115
Chants and text in sense and nonsense 119
Further reading 123

5   Articulation 125

Introduction 125
Articulators 125
Bone prop and how to use it 135
Consonants 137
Patter speak, rap and poetry 147
Further reading 153

6   Resonance 155

Introduction 155
Female and male resonance 159
Accents for musicals 166
Mimicry and impersonations 168
Safe screaming, calling and shouting onstage 171
Further reading 176

Appendix 1: Sample Curriculum 177
Appendix 2: Bibliography and Resources 181
Index 185

Figures

1.1 Ballet shoes   16
1.2 Tap shoes   16
1.3 Character shoes   17
1.4 The human spine   24
1.5 On all fours, spine straight   25
1.6 On all fours, spine dipped   25
1.7 On all fours, spine arched   26
2.1 The ribcage   48
2.2 The vocal folds: with the vocal folds open (A) and
     closed (B)   50
2.3 Inflated and deflated balloons   55
2.4 The diaphragm: showing the diaphragm falling
     (A) and rising (B) on the inhalation and exhalation   57
4.1 Om Mani pandei um: a Buddhist chant   119
4.2 Tomtare twotare torre soh ha: a Hindi chant   119
4.3 Step By Step: a worker's chant   121
4.4 Hey ho hey ya: Navaho tribal chant   121
4.5 Legnei ammarow: a Macedonian student chant   122

Foreword I

During the 55 years that I have been involved in the theatre, both as an actor and a director, I have witnessed many different attitudes towards vocal technique. In voice classes as a student, I was told to use an antiquated method to develop articulation involving a bone prop. This uncomfortable apparatus was balanced between the upper and lower teeth before we embarked on vowel and consonant repetitions, but the exercises were never referred to when it came to working on an actual text.

Attitudes have now changed, and voice work is no longer treated as a separate entity from acting. The actor is encouraged to combine his vocal technique with his character's thought process. The same rule also applies in musical theatre. The songs should arise from the text and the emotional state of the characters, and should help to progress the story rather than halting it. This can only be achieved with good vocal control.

Audibility is now often a problem in the theatre. Drama schools no longer focus on developing the volume and strength of their students' voices, preferring to concentrate on their television technique, given that this may well be the arena that offers the graduates the most work. Straight theatre productions have compensated for the potential lack of vocal stamina in actors by introducing radio microphones, which in turn makes actors lazy in their vocal performances, and unnecessarily reliant on this technological crutch.

If the actor is using his voice properly, there should be no difficulty in him being heard, however large the auditorium, and he should be able to trust that his voice will not fail him, however many shows a week he might need to perform. And although musical theatre performers need radio microphones to be heard above the orchestra, they must always think of their vocal technique as a source of power which the microphone may then enhance, rather than vice versa.

All theatre practitioners will benefit from the clear and practical way that Chris Palmer lays out her principles of vocal technique in relation to musical theatre. The technique is vitally important, but the art is to master it until it seems effortless in performance. Chris will guide the reader unerringly to achieve this effect.

Ian Talbot OBE, Director

Foreword II

As an actor and a performer I have worked in every aspect of show business. I've performed at the RSC, at Shakespeare's Globe, The Royal Exchange, played in intimate spaces such as the Donmar Warehouse and the Almeida, and on film and TV sets around the world. Every aspect of the job requires a knowledge and understanding of how to use and maintain my voice to optimum effect, but none require more care and attention to my vocal performance and strength than working on a musical. Singing professionally takes everything to a more heightened level. Whether it's a week-long workshop of new work (which usually happens when I haven't used my voice for a long period of time) or a year-long run in a commercial musical (when my voice is in peak condition), my voice becomes probably the most important thing I look after, on and off stage. It's mine and makes me the actor I am or the character I want to become, so I take responsibility and have the utmost respect for it. Obviously, singing is different to just talking or shouting (safely), but having a combined knowledge of how to use your voice as a muscle that functions well in peak conditions or under stress and fatigue is what defines a performer who can use technique and instinct to achieve the best results as an actor or triple threat performer.

Use this book, which combines everything needed for a performer or teacher to start at the beginning, or brush up on how you use your muscle, instrument and voice with confidence and conviction.

Michael Jibson, Olivier award-winning actor

Preface for Teachers

This workbook has been a journey I have wished to pursue for many years, understanding the need for a workbook with the sole purpose of bringing together the skills associated for the teaching of voice to the musical theatre performer (MTP) or the creative athlete.

I have been Head of Voice for over 15 years at Guildford School of Acting, University of Surrey, writing voice curricula to meet the demands of the theatrical industry both in acting and musical theatre, whilst maintaining the efficacy and currency of a degree. There are always many challenges to teaching voice and speech, and understanding the differing needs of the MTPs to that of, say, a classically trained actor and is the premise of this book. Whilst performers cross over into the shared world of the theatre, the training is typically different. I have explored at great length the intricacies of singing methodologies, as the innovator and programme leader on the ground-breaking MA Practice of Voice and Singing. The primary aim of this course is to teach vocal coaches to embrace the disciplines of both the singing and the speaking voice, creating a unique vocal coach; one that also incorporates an understanding of dance skills, and has therefore married the voice training to allow an interdisciplinary approach to the skills rather than have them work in opposition.

In my previous vocation as an actress, singer and dancer, I had noticed the varying degrees of opposition regarding the skills of dance, singing and voice, and sought to find commonality.

Through this workbook I have sought to address the balance that will truly allow the triple threat performer to shine.

The language of this workbook is designed to be simple and useful to both teachers and students, alongside those who are interested in musical theatre. Whilst the book is addressed to the performer, there are tips for teachers in each chapter, and suggests that you, the teacher, are able to demonstrate some of the exercises, giving you a greater degree of confidence in teaching some practical voice exercises, whilst understanding the valuable training in dance your students receive.

There are also questions after each chapter for the student, designed to provoke and engage them to think critically about what each exercise has taught them, or question what they feel in terms of their breath or articulation or resonance, and how they perceive or meet each exercise. There may be some exercises that they find physically or vocally demanding, and it is asked that they explore these without judgement of self. There are some exercises for individuals, pairs and groups, and the book is designed to work sequentially, laying the foundations in posture and breath, through to building the voice, pitch range, and articulation and resonance. The young performer whose aim is to work towards voice and speech exams will also find this a most helpful guide to improving their sound and speech quality.

I always advise keeping a voice journal and also keeping recordings of students and clients at the beginning of their training. Dance teachers record their sessions to enable the student to practise the moves, singing teachers record the sessions so that the student may practise with the help of the piano recordings and the exercises. Therefore the voice recordings help the student to hear the vocal shift, even if the true or perceived sound is different in the head than that of the recording.

I hope you will find *Voice and Speech for Musical Theatre* an exciting and new way of voice training, exploring potential, developing stamina and aiding confidence for your students.

Video

Some of the exercises within this workbook can be difficult to explain, therefore the demonstrations of those exercises are best seen and heard. Using two musical theatre students to help demonstrate the exercises, the Video allows you to see what you hope to accomplish with your students and yourself. As the exercises are limited in number, they are there to accompany the workbook, and not in place of the sequential exercises. It may be that you wish to 'flip' the class for a session, a strategy where, as part of your students' homework, you set them the task of watching the exercises on the Video, and familiarizing themselves with the exercise as ground work and then developing the work fully in class, or perhaps using the Video to get your students to teach each other, forming a sense of autonomy. Most of the exercises take much longer in real time than those set out in the Video, as they are there as guidance only and designed to supplement the voice training, not to replace it.

This workbook uses imagery to encourage the imagination by training the body to respond through sensory awareness, by doing and feeling the work first, then through the understanding of why and how the exercises help, with time set for practice and embodying the work further. This, I feel, is especially important to the musical theatre training, as all too often the skills acquired can become a series of drills, and whilst technical and skilful in performance, it has often been said that the MTP can lack emotional connection and truth.

Trained athletes will regularly use imagery in order to focus their minds and engage a positive mental attitude which focuses on attitude and explores imaginative games, alongside their physical training. For me, the MTP is a creative athlete.

Each section will remind the reader of the engagement of good posture and will also show a sequence of vocal exercises associated with exploring the items noted in the chapter heading. As the teacher, you will want to demonstrate the intensity with which you wish them to engage, which will help harness the student's abilities. (Of course, always check for any injuries or breathing issues in advance of any exercises.)

At the end of the Preface for Students I have given a list of learning outcomes which you may find useful.

Finally, a sample curriculum is included that you may find useful, covering two semesters that you can easily adapt to cover a three-term structure.

Preface for Students

Welcome to *Voice and Speech for Musical Theatre*. As one of many creative athletes that line the West End stage and Broadway, I hope you find this book insightful and effective, and that it challenges your voice and creative abilities. I call musical theatre performers (MTPs) creative athletes, which I think you are, as you are expected to sing, dance and act at the same time, all of which require stamina, hard work and discipline, much like an athlete.

This workbook and short Video are designed to show you how to work on your voice individually, or in a group. Each exercise starts from the expectation that your current knowledge of voice work is limited to the spoken voice. It then builds on that foundational knowledge to explore more advanced voice work, designed to enable you to reach your full vocal potential. There is some information on anatomy and physiology and how to use your body most effectively for speech without compromising your dance skills.

You may find some of the exercises overlap a singing lesson or a dance class, and that has been a conscious decision, as it asks you to develop an understanding of the relationship between the three disciplines. This may also help to explain myths surrounding breath support for singing and voice, and core strength and its value in a voice class. This workbook will demystify those burning questions or conflicts and seek to create an understanding of them rather than compromise one skill over another.

All the exercises are clearly laid out for you to explore, both in a class with your tutor, or on your own. You will further develop your vocal range, dexterity and agility, which will help you have a more efficient voice, be a more proficient performer, and will help you extend your performance, offering you the chance to work in a far more healthy and safe manner. To demonstrate the exercises, there is a Video where two MTP students from the musical theatre programme at Guildford School of Acting work through the exercises that we have done many times in class.

This will help you explore some of the exercises correctly and allow you to move through the book, referring back to sections time and again. If you find some exercises challenging then put them to one side and come back to them at a later date. Try to be open to your learning and the process of this workbook. Above all, do not judge yourself or compare yourself to others. This book is aimed at you and your own learning.

I would always recommend keeping a journal of your voice, as this is an excellent way to reflect and record your vocal development. Equally, I recommend recording your speaking voice at the beginning of this workbook and then recording yourself at a later date, when you have worked through the entire book. This will give you an auditory understanding of how much your voice will have advanced and extended. Sometimes it is good to hear your voice without judgement, just acknowledging your voice, where you are now, where you are in one month, in six months and twelve months from now. In your voice journal you could record your thoughts about some of the exercises that have either worked for you, or that you may have found challenging. You will see that there are questions after each chapter to help guide you to what you might wish to write down; you could also record yourself on your phone or a dictaphone on how you feel and sound at the beginning of working through this book and again when you have completed all the exercises by recording yourself again. You should notice a vocal shift and advancement in your abilities, your stamina and your overall sound. I encourage you to speak with passion and joy.

Each section will ask questions of you, which are in italics, such as *how does that feel?* in order for you, the learner, to truly connect with the exercises and become an autonomous learner, rather than always guided by a teacher.

I hope that *Voice and Speech for Musical Theatre* will bring you much success on your journey towards musical theatre and becoming a triple threat performer (an MTP).

Outcomes

The outcomes of this book are to:

- Lay the foundation for a solid technical ability with regard to the spoken voice.
- Develop your personal confidence in speech, text and character work.
- Enhance your understanding of your speaking voice (Social voice).
- Enhance and develop your performance voice (Performative voice).
- Build and integrate performance skills of voice, song and dance (Integrated voice).
- Stimulate a desire for further development, either for personal enjoyment or future professional training (Individual voice).

Acknowledgements

This workbook is a combination of the many people, teachers and practitioners whom I have admired, worked with and trained with over the years. Their inspiration has served to plant the seeds that needed watering and nurturing to grow into the book you hold today. Much of my work is based on their sensibilities as teachers and practitioners and I merely share my own point of view, through the prism of their work, and further advance the principles of teaching voice to the musical theatre performers of the future.

I would like to thank the staff at the Guildford School of Acting who encouraged me and persevered with my incessant talk about this workbook, and special thanks to Sean McNamara Head of Guildford School of Acting, whose leadership allowed my creativity to flourish. I would also like to take the opportunity to thank the artist Jess Hodson Walker, whose drawings made sense of my thoughts; Keith Thomas for his skilled ideas regarding the Video; Dr Marion Heron and her insightful and useful comments on my initial draft; Rachael Kerridge for her wonderful discussions on the subject of dance and core strength; singing teacher Katie Crooks, Nicholas Scrivens and Niall Bailey for their useful insights and general banter; Ben Lewis and Hayden Fletcher, who contributed to the musical scores; and Harry Sheasby and Phoebe Williams, who were instrumental in the making of the Video alongside the help and support for the Video by Harriet Reynolds. I would like to thank all my students past and present, including those on the Voice programme MA in Practice of Voice and Singing, who have been part of the ongoing research, and my partner Christopher Chamberlain whose continuing support is without advertisement.

Finally, thanks to all at Methuen Drama, particularly Lucy Brown, Meredith Benson and Anna Brewer, and the initial encouragement from Camilla Erskine; David Carey for his continuing tutelage long after I was his student and his support as technical editor on this workbook; and copy editor Paul King, for easing my transition into the world of authorship, with clear guidance and honesty.

Introduction

Not long after we are born, we use the body to find sensations, to explore, and to literally find our feet. The physical playfulness of the tongue, the creative sounds we make as a baby, through the babbling qualities, as we vocally explore sounds, are the first steps towards creativity, exploration and communication. This is a new world bathed in light after spending nine months in the womb.

As we grow to stand on our own two feet, to hold our head upright, to view the world above and below, front and back, we further explore life around us. These are generally the first set of learning experiences that we begin to master.

Eventually, standing, walking and talking simultaneously become second nature, as we begin to explore language and patterns of behaviour, which generally serves us for the rest of our lives.

Training the voice for a career in the Performing Arts means returning to the earliest senses of the body, its anatomy and physiology through movement exploration, sensual awareness and creativity, identifying true understanding of the authentic voice as it begins to reveal itself. The poet Henry Longfellow wrote that the 'soul reveals itself through the voice'.

Through exploration comes learning, through learning comes creativity, and through creativity comes understanding of our self. As performers, we take a responsibility to extend the exploration of voice and movement to new and dizzying heights, learning what is vocally possible in a physiological and anatomical sense, and what is possible in an exploratory and creative sense. The creative exploration of vocal skills provides the chance to develop through play, discovery and imagination, without judgement.

The musical theatre performer (MTP) is known as a triple threat athlete (sometimes quadruple threat performer [QMTP] if they play an instrument as well!), where they perform at least three skills to a very high standard. When undergoing musical theatre training in dance, singing and acting, with a range of contradictory directions, the three distinct disciplines can often appear to work in opposition to one another. This workbook aims to bring a more joined-up approach to voice and speech training for the MTP by offering links between speech, song and dance.

This book is suitable for those with an interest in musical theatre and actor musicians, singing teachers who work with MTPs, voice and speech coaches who work with singers, and singers who wish to gain a greater knowledge of the teaching of the spoken voice. It will also be useful to drama teachers and directors of musicals alongside musical directors and choreographers.

If you are a performing arts student, this book will be particularly useful to you as it sets out to explain how voice training can work in conjunction with the two other major skills of singing and dance in an interdisciplinary manner, and offers a link to those skills so that you the student can be a proficient and efficient performer in all three skills.

If you are a performing arts student of musical theatre, wishing to explore musicals or to audition for further training at a conservatoire or other musical theatre institution, this workbook will be most useful to you. It will help you to maximize efficiency in voice, breath, posture and stamina, and further develop the skills required to become a consummate performer, especially for those wishing to be a triple threat within the musical theatre industry.

If you are a drama teacher, voice or singing teacher this workbook offers some suggestions in developing further your practice, offering tips in each chapter, which are designed especially to work for groups. There is also a voice curriculum for a 10-week programme designed to further enhance your practice.

There are many excellent publications and workbooks on each discipline, or even the combination of two disciplines, and some I will refer to. However, there is none that I am aware of that combines all three disciplines and fully integrates the musical theatre training as a collective art form.

***

The MTP generally rehearses musicals differently from the rehearsal of a play. That is not to say the crossover doesn't exist. For example, if a director of plays chooses to direct a musical they will bring their wonderful sensibilities and style to the project, working on the text and characterization. However, for the vast majority of directors and choreographers of musicals, the rehearsal process can often be very different. Often the choreography takes an enormous amount of time within the rehearsal period, and this would suggest that any in-depth character work, or voice and singing technique or accent work is an expectation for which there is little time in the rehearsal process. A prime example of how musicals generally rehearse differently to that of a play may be the use of the mirrors. Performers of musicals can 'see' how it looks, can observe their spacing between one another, in both the dance sequences and the staging, as a dance sequence tells a story in itself, and the performers are able to 'see it' from the audience's perspective. A play is more likely to rehearse without that observation of self, looking inward, as the text and character are worked in finer detail and often in more depth.

An MTP will be trained extensively in one or more of the singing methodologies, including (but not exclusively) the work of Jo Estill with Estill Voice Training (EVT), Seth Riggs and Speech

Level Singing (SLS), or Cathrine Sadolin's Complete Vocal Technique. The body will be trained in ballet, tap and jazz, not to mention contemporary dance, mime work, and mask, and the movement work of Rudolf Laban. The spoken voice pedagogies, meanwhile, reinforce character, place, genre, historical context, accent and clarity, exploring resonance, articulation, posture, breath, speech and accent, and using established voice practitioners such as Cicely Berry, David and Rebecca Clark Carey, Kristin Linklater and Patsy Rodenberg.

These many differing forms create the elements of training for a modern-day MTP, within a conservatoire or like-minded institution in the Performing Arts. Therefore, it is incumbent on teachers to explore the inevitability of a joined-up approach to the training that allows the performer to be the best they can be.

An overview

This book is divided into six chapters, each with subheadings, relating to the foundations of voice training and the interdisciplinary nature of singing, voice and dance. Each chapter will have tips for teachers, which may comment on the work just undertaken, suggest further exercises, or merely offer some advice, including a selection of suggested texts and songs. There is a sample curriculum for a two-semester framework that can easily be adapted to accommodate three terms. The timings and structure indicate a voice lesson undertaken once a week for 2 hours. There is no right way to explore all the differing elements of voice work. However, in line with musical theatre training I have, where possible, aligned the voice work to body, movement, dance and singing, in order to complement the other skills and make reference to them, further enhancing the interdisciplinary nature of this book.

Chapter 1: Posture, Alignment and Neutral Plus focuses on good alignment for voice and speech, and an acknowledgement of what neutral means for the dancer and the singer, and also acknowledging the distinction in posture especially where the three disciplines are in opposition and where they connect. Chapter 2: Breath, Dance and Movement explores breath management, accessing the breath, stamina, core strength, gym and dance breath. Chapter 3: Building the Voice includes the vocal set up from speech to song, intoning and building the voice through archetypes and choral speaking. Chapter 4: Pitch and Tune looks at encouraging pitch range and develops vocal speech variety. Chapter 5: Articulation focuses on diction, patter speak, patter songs, rap and poetry for rapid speed and delivery. Chapter 6: Resonance explores the resonators, placing the sound, accents for musicals, mimicry and impersonations, and finally, calling, safe screaming and shouting.

Each chapter is structured with subheadings that follow a pattern of 'Feel it first' followed by 'Understand it' and finally 'Practise it'. These are followed by sections of suggested texts, songs and further reading. The 'Feel it first' section is just that, exploring through doing and feeling your way through the work; the 'Understand it' sections are about what you have just done, what anatomy may be involved, why the connection is important and hopefully give you some insight if you wish to develop the work further. Finally, the 'Practise it' section offers more exercises for you to explore further. This should deepen your connection to the work having gone through the processes set out earlier.

My philosophy

Learning through doing is the essence of this workbook and if you find that you struggle with an exercise, then leave it alone for a while and come back to it at a later date. There is no rush to get through the exercises, nor should you place any judgements on yourself as you work through the book. The workbook aims to provide you with a greater understanding of the links between training the spoken voice, the singing voice and your dance, allowing you to follow each of the disciplines with a greater degree of acknowledgement of each of these areas.

We all learn in different ways: some of us are keen visual learners, 'I have to see/read it to believe it'; some of us are auditory learners, 'I have to hear it to know I have understood it'; and some of us are kinaesthetic learners, 'I have to feel the work to understand it'. It is a fairly common practice in education to take a holistic approach to teaching, and this more-rounded understanding of education incorporates in a three-way delivery, for you to be truly effective, becoming critical, confident and independent learners. Scientific knowledge alone is no replacement for understanding processes on a kinaesthetic and sensory level, which is why each exercise begins with the kinaesthetic of 'Feel it first'.

I remember one of my mentors explaining a story to me of a competition between an artist and a scientist, where they had to compete in the fastest time ever to climb to the top of a mountain. After many hours of climbing, the artist, who got to the top of the mountain first, shouted down to the scientist on the ledge below, 'What took you so long?' And yet it was Albert Einstein who was believed to have said 'logic will get you from A–Z; imagination will get you everywhere'.

There are many academic studies on assessments and feedback which suggest that tasks that have engaged the body and mind through sensory learning have a greater degree of understanding, and the learning outcomes are far higher and embodied longer to reflect further and enhance learning than that of the academic or narrative approach alone. This book aims to incite passion, determination, problem solving, risk taking, team work and creativity.

Video

This workbook is accompanied by a short Video of some exercises from each chapter, which demonstrate 'how to do' some of the exercises. It is never easy to read an exercise and then try and replicate it, therefore the Video is a guide only. Two musical theatre students, Harry and Phoebe, who have done these exercises many times, demonstrate some of the sequences. The Video that accompanies this book is a guide and cannot take the place of a good voice teacher, but does allow the opportunity to support the workbook in practice. Perhaps you may wish to look at some of the exercises then go back and read the relevant section. A word of caution: if you have any injuries you should make your instructor aware as they will be able to give you safer alternatives. Links to the individual exercises are provided at the back of this book, including a link to all videos.

Further reading

As Isaac Newton said in 1675, 'if I have seen further it is by standing on the shoulders of giants'. I am indebted to all those voice practitioners, movement specialists, singing teachers and actor trainers, who have all in some form shaped how I teach voice and direct, and have further inspired my continual learning. Standing on the shoulders of those 'giants', I have further developed, explored and researched areas based on the work of those practitioners, which will have influenced my style of teaching, and by osmosis helped the development of this book. Each chapter sets out a reading list on some of those practitioners.

Finally, the aim of this workbook is to find voice exercises that will help awaken your love of your speaking voice, to make you cherish the differences between the performative spoken and sung voice, and measure the efficiency to that of your social voice (or your everyday speaking voice) and significantly notice the power and ease of your performative speaking voice. Attributed to the author Malcolm Gladwell in his book *Outliers*, it is said that honing a craft that makes one a master takes roughly 10,000 hours.

Practising the exercises provided is important in order to become a true master of a skill. As Aristotle was reputed to have said, 'we are what we do repeatedly'.

Breathe and enjoy.

1 Posture, Alignment and Neutral Plus

Keywords: awaken, posture, neutral, neutral plus, neutral minus, activate, musical theatre performer (MTP)

> You are cold when you spend so much time looking at the ground, you forget the sun is there to warm you. *NATIVE AMERICAN SAYING*

Introduction

What is considered good posture? What do voice, singing and dance teachers mean when they say 'I want to see you activate the ideal or correct posture' (sometimes known as alignment)? Certainly, I know from my own experience as a singer, dancer and actress that each of these teachers asked me to apply a variety of adjustments in posture, depending on the skill I was working on. Generally, we use the word 'alignment' to understand body use at its most fundamental efficiency, with the engagement of breath management (or breath support), according to the particular skill that is being worked on.

In this chapter, we will develop an understanding of what our bodies are capable of by exploring our habitual posture, and what each discipline for musical theatre training expects from good, efficient and healthy posture. The way we habitually sit or stand has often been in response to how we face the world. It can be because we have poor habits, from carrying heavy bags, to being short (like myself) and thrusting the chin forward, and of course standing in 'good' posture can often make us feel self-conscious, as we expand our chests or stand tall, feeling exposed as if we are baring our bellies. For the musical theatre performer (MTP) in most cases posture and alignment may have been over-corrected in order to fulfil a dance posture criteria, which in turn may have affected the singing or speaking voice through tense muscles in the lower back, belly, legs and buttocks.

The MTP has a range of specialized skills that need to come together fully to perform safely and efficiently, managing their breath and posture to be an effective and healthy performer. Isolating and awakening different parts of the body is fundamental to understanding how the body works and how to continue to reproduce sounds and skills night after night in long-running musicals.

There are many approaches to awaken our understanding of ideal posture or correct alignment, for fluid efficient movement, such as yoga, t'ai chi, pilates, Feldenkrais or Alexander Technique among many others. These skills can also be used for everyday life, but they hold a special place in actor training, and are an excellent accompaniment to the overall training of an MTP. All these practices are about self-observation, in order to adjust or simply notice without judgement what our bodies and voices may 'do' under a relaxed state, an engaged state and a performative state.

When we are young, as in 'baby young', our posture is perceived to be 'correct' in that the stacking of the body parts of feet, knees, hips, ribcage, shoulders, neck and head are in an 'ideal alignment'. Look at a young child of, say, two years of age, sitting on the floor. Their upper body is 'aligned', the stacking of the vertebrae is 'correct' and once they have mastered the weight of the head and neck fully, their body is aligned for optimum use as they awaken the process of walking and talking. Typically, as we get older our bodies change and we start to use our structure in a non-constructive manner. Our interaction with mobile phones, emails, working on computers, laptops or iPads, for example, means we often droop our necks to meet the device, which will inevitably have an impact on our posture. The Alexander Technique is a wonderful way to awaken the 'neutral spine' and engage with effective and efficient posture for voice and speech. Once we have explored neutral, we will move on to look at neutral plus (N+), a term I have devised to investigate the many forms of neutral that the MTP faces. Therefore, to understand the posture of N+, one must first understand the term neutral.

Feel it first

Warm-up (Video)

- Stretch your arms above your head and reach for the sky, clasping your hands together. Keep the shoulders low, then release the arms down.

- Next stretch your arms out to the side and reach for something just beyond your fingertips. Then release the arms down.

- Next flop forward reaching down to the floor and hang there.

- Now slowly come up to standing tall, and stretch again, letting out a yawn.

- Raise your right arm up and stretch over to the other side, then with your left hand pat all over your ribs letting out a sound. Then repeat on the other side.

- Now circle your hips one way, then the other.

- Shake out your arms and hands and let out any sound.

- Now shake out a leg as if a dog has attached itself to you. Say 'get off', and then shake out the other leg as if a tiger is coming at you. Say 'go away'.

- Next shake out your buttocks, and finally shake out the whole body.

- Raise your shoulders and then release them down to a breath or sigh.

- Keeping the chin parallel to the floor, rotate the head by taking the chin slowly over to the left shoulder and then to the right shoulder.

- Take your chin to your chest and circle your nose in a semi-circle from one shoulder over to the other shoulder.

- Give yourself a hug by wrapping your arms around yourself and then bending forward and breathe, letting out a sigh. This will open the back and make you aware of your breath as it moves your ribs and back.

- Circle the foot one way and then the other releasing sound, this could be a hum. Now stand on tiptoe and slowly release your feet down to the floor.

- Now swing your left leg from front to back, always being aware of the breath.

- Now swing your right leg from side to side, again being aware of the breath.

Posture and alignment (Video)

- Stand with your feet in parallel, roughly hip distance apart, the knees should feel soft, as if liquid oil is in the knee joint. Imagine your tailbone or coccyx is hanging down, lengthening in your thoracic spine, and then lengthen the neck vertebrae or (cervical spine) by imagining a balloon attached to the head, feel your head floating upwards away from your body.

- Your neck should feel long, with your head able to nod yes and no. There should be an overall sense of lengthening. The shoulders and arms should hang down by the side, relaxed. The weight ratio should be about 50 per cent at the front of the foot and 50 per cent at the back of the foot, which feels evenly balanced. Now sway back and forwards until you feel balanced in the centre.

This is neutral and the beginning of feeling grounded, centred and aligned.

- Now stand in neutral and feel your body warm, awake and ready.

Understand it

The Alexander Technique arose from the Australian actor F. M. Alexander's desire to analyse and evaluate his own poor vocal technique in performance as an actor. Through observing himself in the mirror he practised his performances, and found his posture was 'out of alignment' (as he put it). He would often thrust his neck forward like a pigeon, and tension would creep into his shoulders, neck and jaw, often causing him to lose his voice. Through this evaluation of self, he mastered an understanding of integrity and efficiency in performance, through working on his posture, and how it should look and what it should feel like, not just for performance but for everyday life. He then began a lifetime dedicated to finding the optimum use of mastering the body for standing, sitting and speaking. Through this intensive period, many others began to accept and adopt the characteristics of what is now known as the Alexander Technique: the study, practice and efficiency of the ideal body alignment.

Many conservatoires and performing arts schools will be aware of the importance and impact his research had, and continues to have, on the training of voice and speech for actor training.

Practise it

- Begin by standing with your feet together and rigid like a soldier.
- Now stand with your legs apart, slumped over as if you are a really cool dude.

- Next try standing in neutral as you did earlier. *How does it feel?*
- Now let's repeat the routine whilst walking, so try walking around the room rigid as a soldier. *Does this feel tense?*
- Now walk around the room as you would normally, and then stop still. *How does the walk feel?*
- Next try walking around the room in neutral. *How does this feel?*
- Now walk around the room slumped like a cool dude, and then stand still. *How does the walk feel?*
- Again walk around the room neutral. *Does neutral feel more appealing?*
- Stand in neutral.

Can you feel the differences in each physical state?

Are you able to feel the difference in your breath or tension in your body?

Do you feel like a different character?

What is the energy like as you walk and then stand still?

Does neutral feel more natural now?

Tips for teachers

The MTP lives and breathes so much physical work, in ballet, tap and jazz that a moment of calm reflection before beginning voice work is more beneficial than racing in to cover a curriculum. This also provides a moment to scan the body, connecting to the breath. For this I prefer to use the first part in each session to have the students lying on the floor with the legs raised against a wall. The buttocks can be lifted on to a block so that they feel higher than the heart. This in yoga is known as an 'adrenal dump', to allow time to focus on the breath, to relax the feet and legs, and allow time to rest and bring the body to a state ready for voice work, free from presentation. This should take about 3 minutes. Then I feel the students are ready to work on their voices. (Whilst cardiovascular work is such a large part of the training of an MTP, I often refrain from spending too much time on such work.) However, it is important to feel energized in a voice class and therefore some running, jumping and arm swinging can be a useful way to begin. If the students have come from a dance class, then ending your warm-up being centred and aligned in neutral posture is also a positive way to begin the voice work.

Neutral plus (N+): The foundations, feet first and the body

The term neutral plus refers to a good working posture used between the singing pose and neutral pose used in voice class for correct alignment. As you know when you sing, you may be asked to hold your chest high, stand with one foot forward, lean back or stand in neutral. Yet N+ allows you to feel the areas of posture associated with the technical skills of singing. Later in this chapter, we shall also look at neutral minus, often used in dance.

In order to explore N+ it is useful to engage the body from the feet upwards in detail; therefore, from the feet, through the knees, hips, spine, ribs, shoulders to the neck, we will fully explore the whole body.

Feet

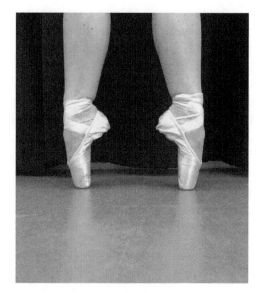

Figure 1.1 Ballet shoes.

Figure 1.2 Tap shoes.

Figure 1.3 Character shoes.

Look at your feet, and the various shoes you will wear throughout your musical theatre career: from ballet shoes and en pointe, to tap shoes, jazz shoes, character shoes and some shoes that are 3 inches high, causing all manner of blisters and bunions. The ball of the foot and the big toe have a great deal of pressure put upon them. Let's be honest, dancers' feet are some of the most tired that we will see; they are working feet! The feet of a dancer must withstand the physical demands of constant dancing through rehearsals and performance and the shoes worn will have an impact on the posture, especially moving from speech to song. Exploring the body upwards from your foundations will secure the building blocks into N+.

***

For the following, you will need a pen, a stone and other objects both hard and soft, or perhaps even a banana. (A prickle ball, for example, is fine.) You will need to sit on a chair with your feet flat on the floor, book or block.

Feel it first

- Let us begin by looking down at your feet, and separate each toe. You may have to actively separate each toe with your fingers, as if you are having a pedicure.
- Now raise your toes up and gently place them down.
- Now stretch your toes out as if you were a cat.
- Now raise and lower the arches of each foot whilst keeping your toes and heels on the floor.
- Now tuck the toes under your feet then release them.

Tips for teachers

Rehearsing in character shoes can often be tiring and therefore students should take time to release the muscles in the feet, which can help rebalance the energy in the whole body. The toe tuck and feet stretching is very useful and you could combine a release of tension in the jaw with the students self-massaging their feet. Recognizing the symmetry between discomfort and tension and how to help isolate and release that will give them tools to discover this further autonomously.

Practise it

- Stand on tiptoe and balance there for a moment.
- Stand on tiptoe, then release the heels down slowly to the floor and feel as many muscles in your feet, knees and legs as you can.
- Stand on a book or a block with your heels hanging onto the floor so that only the front of your foot is on the block. Note how the muscles in the legs work and how

hard the toes work, and how your balance is affected. Now try the same exercise with your heels on the block and your toes on the floor.

- Now, keeping on the tiptoes, reduce the heels down to 50 per cent.
- Next drop your heels suddenly in a heel tap.
- Repeat this heel tap several times.
- Now, with one foot pick up a pen, a stone or other small object.
- Repeat the same exercises with the other foot.
- Now see if you can pass the object to someone else.
- In a circle, pass around an object with the foot such as a stone, placing the object in front of another person. Then, to make it more difficult, pass the stone from foot to hand in pairs.
- The 3-minute writing challenge: Take a felt-tip pen or a piece of chalk and write a word or perhaps a sentence using only the foot, on the floor or on a large piece of paper.

Understand it

Whilst it is reasonable to explore voice work in bare feet, at some point voice training should incorporate the wearing of dance shoes and especially heels. Wearing heels improves the MTP's understanding of back muscle engagement, and therefore, in some voice classes, the wearing of shoes is encouraged, both for male and female. Men play a vast range of female roles in musicals, *Hairspray*, *The Stripper*, *Toxic Avenger* and *Kinky Boots* to name a few, and all these characters require shoes in rehearsals as well as performance; therefore a voice class in heels can help integrate the vocal and physical demands of a show in high shoes.

Knees

Feel it first

Knees (Video)

- Begin by standing in neutral and check that the knees feel soft, like liquid oil is inside the knee joint.

- Now bend the knees.

- Next bounce up and down, releasing a 'huh' sound on each bounce.

- Next try a double bounce 'huh, huh', 'huh, huh'. Once again bounce up and down bending at the knees counting aloud from 1 to 10.

Tips for teachers

Any of the knee exercises must be done with care, and those with knee injuries or ongoing knee problems should avoid this exercise. Dancers can often have shin splint injuries, so they may have special exercises to do which can be accommodated here.

Practise it

Place your hands on your knees and circle them clockwise and then anti-clockwise. In pairs, assign a voice to a partner's knees, such as an 'old lady's voice' or a 'little boy's voice' and allow your partner to draw a face on your knee (not in indelible marker). Each pair draws a face on their partner's knees and then they begin a conversation; they can then move around the room having many conversations. Repeat the exercise with the other leg changing partners. Have your own knees talk to each other in the mirror.

Understand it

This allows you to feel knee engagement, to understand the knees especially for jumps, lifts, turns and pirouettes; giving care to those moving parts of the knees encourages gentle awareness in this area and it's also a bit of fun.

Hips

Feel it first

Hips 1: Hindi squat (Video)

- From the standing neutral pose, take your legs wide apart with your feet slightly splayed and your toes pointing out so that the hips are more open.

- Bend at the knees and release your hips down to the floor, in a squat position, known as the Hindi squat pose in yoga.

- Bring your elbows inside of the thighs and lightly push them towards your thighs. Mark the beginning of the pose with an exhalation. If you feel you are falling forward then move against a wall for some support. If your heels do not reach the floor, do not place any judgement on yourself, just put a block or a book under your heels; this will help you stay in this position.

- Slowly bend forward bringing your feet together and uncurl your spine, so that you are standing once again in an upright position in neutral.

Hips 2: Happy baby pose with babbling baby (Video)

- Lie on the floor on your back, and bring your knees to your chest. Grip your feet or lower leg with your hands. Keep your head, shoulders and back on the floor. You can use a belt or hold the lower part of your legs.

- Open the legs wide so that your knees are as wide as your shoulders, if you can. Mark the beginning of the pose with an exhalation.

- Breathe in and out and relax in this position. Start timing this pose beginning with 30 seconds, then release. Increase this pose to a maximum of 3 minutes. If you need to release the hold then just bring the feet together for a moment; this still activates the hips and relaxes the legs. As you remain in this position, relax the jaw and tongue. If you need a block under your head then do so, as this will prevent the activation of the shoulders or the head and the neck wishing to move off the floor. Continue breathing in and out for 1 minute to allow time to release the hips, jaw and tongue.

- In this same position begin to hum for a full 1 minute.

- Continuing in happy baby pose, open your mouth and make the AH vowel sound. Do this for a full 1 minute.

- Continue in baby pose and place your tongue behind the bottom teeth and release the tongue in and out much like a baby. Release legs out by lying flat on your back and have a full body stretch releasing a sigh.

Hips 3: Wide legged extended child's pose (Video)

- Begin by kneeling down on the floor and sit back on your heels, with your feet flat on the floor, and take your knees far apart, allowing your hips to open and your belly to relax to the floor, taking your arms as far as they go to the floor. If you need a block or cushion for your head then do so.

- Mark the start of this position with an exhalation, as you relax into this position for 1 minute.

- Continue with this position and begin to hum, keeping the jaw open and relaxed with the lips gently closed. Hold this for 1 minute.

Understand it

Why does opening the hips mean so much to the voice? Tight ligaments in the hips create tension, both down towards the knees, legs and feet, and in the upper body, with tension in the abdomen and as far up as the jaw, as well as affecting breathing. The hips are made up of fascia and ligaments, much like the pith of an orange. To hold an orange together, that pith is strong, much like the fascia of your hips. Activation of blood to the hips through breath work in long yoga holds releases the connective fascia, and lengthens the fibrous tissue, allowing for strength and flexibility. To maintain and manage that flexibility, releasing into long holds of the positions outlined above improves your range of motion, and provides a deeper connection to your breath, reminding yourself to relax the jaw at regular intervals.

If these ligaments are not released, then over time they become very strong, causing all manner of pain in the hips and other joints and can reduce the flexibility in this area, creating a negative effect on your posture, and therefore your voice. The hip area and psoas muscle can also, according to some yoga practitioners, hold emotional tension and is often known as where the 'soul resides'. The vocal aim of doing these poses is to encourage relaxation of the tongue and jaw, and they are adapted from Yin Yoga exercises for breath release, jaw relaxation, tongue release and sound.

Practise it

Regularly practise hip openers, exploring breath (both noisy breath release and quiet breath release).

Spine

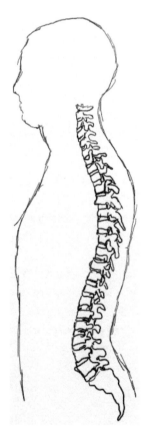

Figure 1.4 The human spine.

Feel it first

- Begin by kneeling on all fours, feel your shoulders moving back towards your feet and breathe in and out as if your back were a table, nice and flat.

Figure 1.5 On all fours, spine straight.

- Now breathe in as you lift the tailbone and the head, creating a slight dip or curve in your spine. Think of yourself as a cow. Moo like a cow.

Figure 1.6 On all fours, spine dipped.

- Now as you breathe out, activate the core muscles towards the spine, as your back becomes arched. Think of yourself as an angry cat, and meow like a cat.

Figure 1.7 On all fours, spine arched.

- Release back to the table-top position. Repeat the sequence of cow to table to cat as many times as you need to feel your spine release.
- Now move your tailbone from side to side so that your whole spine moves snake-like.
- Move the hips in a circle clockwise using the breath. Repeat the exercise in an anti-clockwise motion using the AH vowel sound.
- Now lie flat on your back in supine. Feel the weight of your body relax into the floor.

Understand it

The spine is made up of four areas: the sacral spine which sits between the two hip bones and is found behind the pelvis; the lumbar spine, which carries most of the body's weight and is therefore where lower back problems occur; the thoracic spine, which connects to the ribs, giving it strength; and the cervical spine, located in the neck area and a very important region which protects the brain stem and the spinal cord as well as supporting the skull.

The word SUPINE is only a U away from SPINE! We use the term semi-supine in voice classes. The word supine means to lie flat and therefore semi-supine means to lie *half flat*. It should be done lying on the floor with your feet flat on the floor and your knees bent. We lie on the floor in semi-supine to allow the back to engage with the floor. The support of the floor allows time for the body to become grounded, centred and aligned. The floor acts as a guide on how the body may feel in the upright position, allowing you to feel the natural curve of your spine and release tension in your shoulders, back and buttocks.

This kind of floor work is especially useful for the MTP as so much of training is responding to the exciting demands of all the other disciplines. Floor work allows time to assimilate the other work, can be positive for back and hips and truly allows a connection to the earth.

Practise it

- Lie flat on your back on the floor. Here you are supine.
- Now bend your knees, keeping your feet flat on the floor. Now you are in semi- supine.
- Tilt the pelvis back and forth as far as it goes whilst keeping your buttocks on the floor and find the midway point, and settle there.
- Whilst keeping your head on the floor, tilt your head back and forth, so that your chin moves from ceiling to chest. Then find the midway point, and settle there.
- Some of you may need a book or block for your head as your chin might need to tuck in ever so slightly.
- Relax your arms down by your sides with the palms facing upwards. Now breathe in and out and feel the body relax in semi-supine.

Ribs

Feel it first

Banana stretch or half-moon rib stretch (Video)

- Lie on your back on the floor with your legs outstretched and your arms above your head.

- Now bring yourself into a half-moon shape, or a banana shape, by taking your legs and arms over to one side. Try to keep both buttocks on the floor, and keep both shoulders on the floor. You will imagine that you look like a banana or a half-moon. A curve in your body will occur; notice the stretch in your ribs and spine.

- Mark the beginning of the pose with an exhalation.

- Return to supine (completely flat) and stretch, and release on a sigh.

- Repeat on the opposite side, then come back to supine (lying flat on the floor and relax your legs outstretched).

Understand it

This is a wonderful way to stretch the body down the whole side. It stretches the oblique stomach muscles and the intercostal muscles between the ribs. The MTP dances hard and this stretch, whilst having physical benefits of a good stretch, is also claimed to work on the heart and lungs, creating space.

Practise it

Practising this daily for 3 to 5 minutes and then a counter posture of happy baby pose, or hugging the knees to massage the lumbar area, will also have the beneficial effect of working on the gall bladder meridian for those interested in the acupressure points.

Feel it first

Sphinx (Video)

- Lie on your front and take your arms to shoulder height, with your forearms flat out in front of you, so that you feel like the image of a cactus tree.

- Take your legs long and slightly wider than hip distance apart. This will stop you activating your lower back and buttocks.

- Raise your upper body up, keeping your arms bent at the elbow, so that you feel and look like a sphinx. Mark the beginning of the pose with an exhalation. Hold the pose for 1 minute and breathe.

- Lie on your front and put both arms down by your side, placing your head to the left for 30 seconds, then repeat on the other side. This will release the neck.

- Now repeat the sphinx pose and hum for 1 minute. Lie on your front and release the neck on both sides as before.

- Release your arms down to the floor, this time by your side, release the neck and shoulders turning your head to one side, then to the other.

Understand it

Practising the sphinx pose lengthens the abdominal muscles and is perfect accompaniment after working in a dance class. Whilst it is a back bend that works on the spine, opens the chest and lungs, it also calms the nervous system and is very good for fatigue.

Practise it

The sphinx pose is one to practise daily, always mindful to take the legs wide and resist activating the thighs and buttocks. I would suggest 2 minutes in this pose as it also can help with fatigue. If you feel up to it and know your body is capable, you could move into seal pose, which means you merely straighten your arms. Seal is not for everybody.

Feel it first

Curling and uncurling (Video)

Going down:

- Standing in the neutral position, have your feet hip distance apart, allow your chin to drop to your chest, and feel the weight of the head as it brings your spine forward and down. Allow your legs to slightly bend at the knees, as you release the shoulders and as you continue to move forward and downwards, so that you are hanging down.
- Mark the pose with an exhalation and a sigh.

Coming up:

- When you feel ready to stand upright you will need to uncurl your spine, very slowly.
- Aim to activate the core muscles, as you begin to uncurl your spine and come to an upright position. Leave the chin on the chest, as you come to a standing position, and then slowly raise the chin and head.
- Repeat this sequence several times, perhaps to some gentle music.
- Notice your breathing, then walk around the room, and notice how you feel.

Understand it

All these exercises for the spine – from the cat–table–cow sequence, via the rib stretch of the banana, extending to the sphinx pose and finally the curling and uncurling sequence – help demonstrate the importance of the spine. Your awareness of it through this work establishes connection to your posture. The curling and uncurling of the spine can be done to music and can bring a positive energy to the room, requiring the students to engage with the spine with integrity. The eyes should remain open, as the deep breath work that accompanies this could cause some dizziness. Some imagery I use for the curling and uncurling of the spine includes: a bicycle chain; a glow of light up and down the spine; a string of pearls from head to foot; or a gold thread. But of course you may choose your own. I would suggest you demonstrate the exercises where possible as you become the visual aid for your students.

Tips for teachers

Cat–table–cow is an ideal back stretch, as it awakens and isolates the spine. The sphinx is a wonderful exercise for upper body work and isolation, relaxing the glutes or the buttocks for dancers can be difficult and requires time to allow this to release.

Practise it further

Opening and closing sequence (Video)

For further work on the spine, I have devised an exercise sequence called 'the opening and closing sequence' which you will find on the Video. This works very well as an aid to feeling the connection to the spine and deepens the connection to breath and sound. It is a good sequence to explore, and can be done to music.

- Begin by standing in neutral posture, arms down by the side, and then curl the spine downwards so that your head is the first to release down.

- Then kneel to prayer or extended child's pose.

- Next turn onto one side into a foetus pose, then open the legs so that you are on your back and imagine you are an oyster shell. Stay there for a moment.

- Then close the legs or shell on the other side, and you will be in foetus pose again.

- Next move into the extended child's pose or prayer.

- Then curl the toes and push onto your feet, and finally uncurl the spine, leaving the chin on the chest as it is the last to come up.

Shoulders: The top line

What is a top line? This is when the shoulders are aligned, the neck is long and the arms have fluidity and grace. The arms and shoulders should feel engaged without tension: long loose arms should feel light, and the shoulders should feel activated, moving down and back towards your spine. You can do this whilst looking in a mirror. Always be aware of your top line, and notice if you are balanced in both shoulders. If you play any instruments, you may find the shoulder alignment is off balance. Use the mirror or a partner to correct any imbalance. The neck should feel long, and the chin should be parallel to the floor with your sight line raised rather than straight ahead.

Feel it first

- Look in a full-length mirror.
- Balance your shoulders.
- Breathe in, feel a lift in the lowest ribs as they move away from the hips whilst keeping the shoulders down and back.
- Imagine you have angel wings.
- Imagine your head floating upwards, and your lowest ribs floating upwards away from your hips.

- Raise and drop your shoulders.
- Inhale, and then exhale.

Neck, chin and head release
Feel it first

- Stand or sit with your spine in neutral.
- With your chin parallel to the floor, turn your head very slowly to the right shoulder and stay there for 10 seconds.
- Now bring your head back to centre, then turn your head to the left shoulder, still keeping your chin parallel to the floor, and keep there for 10 seconds.
- Allow your head to return to the centre.
- Now tilt your head to the right as if resting your right ear on your shoulder and let it rest there for 10 seconds. Now bring your head back to centre, tilt the chin to the left shoulder for 10 seconds, and bring back your head to centre.
- Now drop your chin to your chest and leave there for 10 seconds. Then come back to centre.
- Now raise your chin to the ceiling, keeping a long front throat and neck, stay there for 10 seconds, and allow your head to come back to centre.
- Now drop the chin to the chest again and rest there for 10 seconds.
- Next place two fingers in the small crevice between the back of your head and neck (known as the suboccipital triangle) in the base of the skull. Push against it with your head and neck. Try to keep the rest of the body in neutral and relaxed; this will engage the sternocleidomastoids. This is a pair of the largest cervical muscles, which are visible when rotating your head to the left or right; they

are like thick straps that support the neck. When you rotate the neck to the left, you can see the muscle as it flexes on the right side, and when you rotate the neck to the right you can see the muscle flex on the left.

- The chin should raise ever so slightly so that you can imagine a large C from chin to chest, to do this make your hand into a large C-shape. Let the chin rest on your fingers and the thumb rest on your chest. The neck should feel long and floating upwards towards the sky, with the head resting on the top, capable of nodding no and yes.

How does it feel? How does it feel to isolate the neck and head? Are you more conscious of your head on top of your spine?

Understand it

The release of the neck muscles cannot be emphasized enough. Singers, dancers and musicians can have a lot of tightness and rigidity in this area, which in turn affects the jaw and tongue muscles, causing unnecessary tension and potentially leading to all sorts of vocal problems. The neck muscles from the shoulders and from the jaw (sternocleidomastoids) can become very tight due to over 'anchoring' in singing (a term often used to activate these muscles in order to hold the larynx in neutral); this can shorten the suboccipital area. Releasing tension in this area daily will allow you to engage those muscles with less effort and give you the right amount of tension needed for any sense of the 'singing set up'.

Practise it

- Standing in neutral, take your right arm and stretch it up, placing the arm over your head towards your left ear. Without pulling down hold the arm there for 15 to 20 seconds.

- Repeat on the other side.

- Taking your left ear over to the left shoulder, take your right arm and stretch it away. You will feel a slight pull on your neck, to release the tension.

- Repeat on the other side. Now that the body is fully awake from feet to head we can engage with the N+.

Tips for teachers

Tension in the shoulders and neck can very quickly manifest itself in the jaw and tongue. Massaging into this area can be very useful and I would suggest the 'massage line' if you have odd numbers in the class, then perhaps 'pair peer massage' if you have even numbers. This allows the students to feel their tension and gives them solutions to solving the issue. I would suggest the head and neck release should be part of a daily routine.

The postural changes: For speech, song and dance

Neutral plus (N+)

Feel it first

Neutral plus (N+) (Video)

- Begin by standing in neutral.

- Next take your legs wider apart, standing with your feet slightly turned out, this should feel like a wider stance than the neutral posture.

- Bend the knees slightly.

- Now feel that the weight ratio is 55 per cent at the back of your feet and 45 per cent at the front of your feet. It may feel like you want to fall slightly as you lean backwards.

- Option 1. Place two fingers in your suboccipital area (the fleshy bit at the base of your skull) and push against this.

- Option 2. Place your forefinger on the middle of your forehead and push against it. This will engage your sternocleidomastoids, as you find some resistance. Once you have felt this resistance, drop your arms to the side.

- Raise your lowest rib away from your hips by lifting the chest, and lengthen your torso.

- Lengthen in the neck.

- Place your hand on your chest in the shape of a big C, with your thumb on your chest and your chin leaning gently on your four fingers. This creates the shape of the letter C.

This creates the correct posture for N+.

Understand it

I use the term neutral plus merely to distinguish when moving from speech to song. It is meant as a *framework* for understanding the other important disciplines that make up an MTP, and is in addition to what is already understood in terms of the neutral posture, rather than instead of it. I was conscious for many years that MTPs shifted their posture when moving from speech to song in order to get the right 'set up' for the song they were about to perform. There was often the tendency to shorten the suboccipital muscles, especially when going for the 'money note', and jutting the chin forward and upwards. Realizing this was a common phenomenon amongst singers, I observed the posture changes depending on the kind of singer they were.

For example, if they had come from a more traditional operatic background, the natural standing posture tended to be in the Bel Canto mode, of one foot slightly forward and the hips much wider apart, with the ribcage held high. If singers were 'belting' songs, then I noticed the legs would often be too bent, leaning back and locked. I often saw soprano singers with tension in the buttocks, and further to that, bass and baritone singers who would tuck the chin down and flare out the back muscles. Whilst it is generally recognized that the FACH system of voice classification exists, there is substantial crossover of performers from opera to operetta, for example, or from rock and pop music to musicals, and the posture for each genre is different. MTPs are required to work across genres with more fluidity. Therefore, understanding neutral and its brother N+ and sister neutral minus (see below) will help the performer, as they move from style to style; after all, performing in *Showboat* is different to performing in *Bat out of Hell*.

N+ can also be utilized on occasion in order to feel the difference in weight ratio and activation of muscles between singing and dance. It complements the other skills rather than fighting with them. However, these are used in a class merely for awakening the imagination and not for any performance purposes.

The place to engage with N+ is in a technical or practical voice class. It is useful to feel the body weight shift from neutral to N+, back and forth, to engage and activate various muscles and to also acknowledge when you are 'overdoing it'. N+ would not be used in performance, much like the 'neutral'. It is an investigation into the range of muscles associated with singing and speaking, noticing what the body and voice are 'doing'. The slight leaning back is often used in some technical singing lessons with the chin slightly lifted as if looking towards the top row of an auditorium in a theatre. Having a good or correct 'top line' by drawing the shoulders back and down is used in dance.

Practise it

- Place your forefinger on the middle of your forehead and push against it. This will engage your sternocleidomastoids.

- Stand with your feet flat and your toes spread, and imagine your knees are liquid oil. Relax the buttocks, and feel a widening in the hips.

- Imagine the lowest ribs floating upwards, and feel a length in the spine.

- Check that your chin is parallel to the floor, and your shoulders should aim to be down and back (think of relaxed angel wings). Your head should feel it is floating upwards, and your eye line gaze slightly upwards.

- Make a large C with your hand, with the thumb on your chest and the rest of the hand resting under your chin.

- Take your weight slightly forward (N–). Then balance the weight in the centre (neutral). Now lean slightly back (N+).

- Speak a line of text from a poem or sonnet in neutral.

- Now speak a line of text from a sonnet or a poem in N+.

How does it feel?

Explore the neutral and N+ with speech, then move to a song, then back to speech; at this stage don't worry about any accents, although if you want to try then have a go.

How does it feel to take your weight into the three areas?

What muscles are engaged?

Do you feel tall?

Do you feel wide?

Tips for teachers

To think creatively about N+, I use the image of lightly
squeezing oranges or melons under the armpits, to
engage the back muscles, as if activating in a downwards
motion. The shoulder scapulae should be moving down
towards the back of the spine. This will lift the ribcage,
engaging the internal intercostal muscles, so that when
breath is inspired the abdomen does not need to be
consciously engaged, instead it becomes a by-product of
the breath in, and this in turn will naturally allow for a
more freely abdominal space.

Neutral minus (N–)

Feel it first

- Begin by standing in neutral.

- Take your weight over the feet to the front of the foot, to
  the balls of the feet. Imagine your energy is coming out
  through the top of the head, and yet the balls of the
  feet have to move through the floor. You will feel the
  calves working very hard indeed, and will no doubt
  have experienced this in a jazz warm-up. Well done:
  you are in neutral minus (N–).

- Now rock backwards, so that your weight ratio means
  you are now back in neutral.

- Next roll forward again for N–, then rock back to the
  middle for neutral.

- Now feel the weight ratio as you move slightly
  backwards into N+.

Can you feel the weight ratio between these two physical states?

How does it feel?

What is your breath doing in each posture?

How does it feel to take your weight into the two areas of N– and N+?

What muscles are engaged?

Does your neck feel longer at the back as your shoulders move downwards?

Do you feel tall?

Do you feel wide?

Understand it

If there is a neutral plus then surely there is a neutral minus! I would suggest that any dancer would know the energy and commitment placed in the body on the front of the feet in dance. The weight ratio in much of dance will be on the balls of the feet, the toes and the ankles, especially in jumping, where the dancer needs to exercise more force in order to counteract their own body weight in order to jump upwards. I define the three separate neutrals, of neutral, N+ and N– in order to experience the energy shift of front, middle and back of the feet.

Practise it

Once you have begun to experience the differences in the postures, go back and analyse and explore them more fully, so that you begin to have muscle memory. Take the rock and roll exercises as part of a warm-up, where you develop an understanding of how your body becomes more efficient for the task that is required, and interpret and extend that skill further. Developing all the neutrals, from N– to N+.

- Start in neutral and voice a AH vowel sound.
- Roll forward to N– and voice a AH vowel sound.
- Rock back to N+ and let out a AH vowel sound.

- Speak the text below: it is the first chorus speech from *Henry V* by William Shakespeare. Speak the text in neutral posture, then go back and try it in N+, and then finally move to N–.

O for a muse of fire, that would ascend
The brightest heaven of invention,
A kingdom for a stage, princes to act,
And monarchs to behold the swelling scene!
Then should the warlike Harry, like himself,
Assume the port of Mars; and at his heels,
Leash'd in like hounds, should famine, sword and fire
Crouch for employment. But pardon, gentles all,
The flat unraised spirits that have dared
On this unworthy scaffold to bring forth
So great an object. Can this cockpit hold
The vasty fields of France? Or may we cram
Within this wooden O the very casques
That did affright the air at Agincourt?
O, pardon, since a crooked figure may
Attest in little place a million,
And let us, ciphers to this great account,
On your imaginary forces work.
Suppose within the girdle of these walls
Are now confined two mighty monarchies,
Whose high upreared and abutting fronts
The perilous narrow ocean parts asunder.
Piece out our imperfections with your thoughts.
Into a thousand parts divide one man,
And make imaginary puissance.
Think, when we talk of horses, that you see them
Printing their proud hoofs i'th' receiving earth.
For 'tis your thoughts that now must deck our kings,
Carry them here and there, jumping o'er times,
Turning th' accomplishment of many years
Into an hour-glass: for the which supply,
Admit me Chorus to this history,

Who prologue-like your humble patience pray,
Gently to hear, kindly to judge our play.

What do you notice in all three neutrals?

How does your voice and body feel?

We shall look further at these postures and how it affects the breath in the next chapter.

Suggested texts

Here are some suitable texts for you to try:

Carol Ann Duffy, 'Meeting Midnight'
Gerard Manley Hopkins, 'Peace'
Alice Oswald, 'Wedding'
William Shakespeare, *Henry V* chorus speeches
William Shakespeare, Sonnets 22, 27 and 54

Further reading

Bain, K. (2015), *The Principles of Movement*, London: Oberon Books.

Bainbridge, C. B. (1994), *Sensing Feeling and Action*, Berkeley, CA: North Atlantic Books.

Carey, D. and R. Carey Clark (2008), *Vocal Arts Workbook and DVD*, London: Methuen Drama.

Duffy, C. A. (2009), *New Collected Poems for Children*, London: Faber and Faber.

Leborgne, W. and M. Daniels Rosenberg (2014), *The Vocal Athlete*, San Diego, CA: Plural Publishing.

Long, R. (2008), *The Key Poses of Yoga*, Baldwinsville, NY: Bandha Yoga Publication.

Newlove, J. (1993), *Laban for Actors and Dancers*, London: Nick Hern Books.

Nicholls, C. (2008), *Body, Breath and Being: A new guide to the Alexander Technique*, Hove: D and B Publishers.

Shakespeare, William (2010), *The Complete Works of Shakespeare*, London: Arden.

2 Breath, Dance and Movement

Keywords: harmony, activate, breath management, core strength

When the music changes so does the dance. *AFRICAN PROVERB*

Introduction

What is breath management or breath control? What does a voice, singing or dance teacher mean by this statement? Breath management, breath control or breath support is understanding how to use your breath for the task required. This chapter will explore breath for voice, breath for song and breathing for dance or movement, including how it is accessed, what muscles are activated, and how core strength can affect the breath. It further sets out to guide the reader to develop an understanding of the differences of breath management in relation to all three disciplines of dance, singing and voice, by exploring breath support for speech, especially after a movement or dance sequence which leads to song or back to speech. The chapter also sets out to establish the relationship with the body and the voice and to affect afficiency of breath with the dance skills expected.

There is a saying in the classical singing world that 'they who know how to breathe and pronounce well, know how to sing and speak well'. This term has been attributed to the castrato singer and teacher Gasparo Pacchierotti, and the music historian

Charles Burney is believed to have said: 'it is one thing to breathe, another to vocalize that breath'. These are just some statements that are made in relation to the singing voice, the spoken voice and breath itself. It goes without saying that performance in speech, song and dance requires more breath than in everyday social life.

The primary concern of the muscles for breathing is to keep us alive. However, breath is also emotional, instinctive, and our breath reveals a great deal about how we interact with the world, such as thoughts, feelings and ideas. Our out-breath is important for our communication, responses or withholding of thoughts. The breath used for singing, speaking, playing a wind instrument; to dance, run, or swim is the same breath, it just requires a managed use of that breath, and an understanding of how to utilize the breath for maximum efficiency. In this chapter we will see how we can use the breath for speech in a musical after dancing.

You may well have seen the BBC TV programme *Strictly Come Dancing* in Britain (*Dancing with the Stars* in the USA, *Let's Dance* in Sweden, and *Skal vi Danse* in Norway), and can immediately notice that once the dancing is finished how hard the dancers are breathing, as the comments from the judges come through. Imagine having to dance and sing or dance then speak as you would in a musical; only then does it become apparent that the focus on breath and the effort required is substantial.

Breath management and stamina

Using a warm-up that requires both gentle movement of body and breath work, engaging the mind almost meditatively, is a good way to focus the breath.

T'ai chi sequence (Video – a sample of each movement and breath sequence only)

This inspired t'ai chi sequence has been adapted so that the movements and the names are given in English, with sounds which build as the sequence develops, and is designed to establish breath, sound and movement together. The flow of the movement sequences and breath should work together, leading to sound which becomes a sustained intoning. The intention is to access breath that encourages and accompanies the movement sequence. When the movement stops, so should the breath or sound, and I would encourage an equal amount of repetitions on both sides for each movement sequence.

Feel it first

Sequence 1 with breath **(see Video for detail of movements)**.

- The archer for 1 minute.
- Stroking the horse's back for 1 minute.
- Separating the clouds for 1 minute.
- Gazing up at the moon for 1 minute.
- Push the dragon away for 1 minute.

Repeat the sequence above with sound as set out below.

Sequence 2 with a sustained sound of the HUM for 2 minutes.

Sequence 3 with AH vowel for 2 minutes.

Sequence 4 intoning a sustained note on the OO vowel for 2 minutes.

Sequence 5 intoning on the consonant sound SH for 2 minutes.

This sequence is a great way to warm up the body and voice. It is also a wonderful way to cool down after much exertion, for example after a song and dance sequence, taking the sequences in the opposite order, bringing the body back to the breath. It allows you to connect with movement and breath and take time to settle.

Understand it

When we are simply breathing in and out, breath for life is an unconscious action. It becomes conscious when we have to think about our breath for a physical task or performing in speech and song. *'Do I have enough breath for the length of phrase?' 'Can I breathe in the middle of a line, as the musical phrase suggests a breath here, but the text really suggests I breathe then?'* This is when we become conscious of our breath and breath management. However, conversely, this conscious breathing for speech and song can often create panic, stress and tension; in fact, we stop trusting our breath management when we have to speak lines, especially long thoughts, and this adds to our feelings of panic. Breath for sound, breath for action, reaction and impulse added to a range of movements and emotions, needs to be consciously met, understood, and acted upon. Therefore, knowing you have been breathing fine all your life is a start; trust that you already know how to breathe, but are now looking for ways to sustain thoughts, create volume and pitch and tune. That's all – we are just looking to extend your breath and how to use it for more than a social setting, for performance. This is what is different in breath management than it is for most other people. The training of the MTP is like training for the Olympics: they are creative athletes and the breath is a prime example of this training. More oxygen is needed for dance than for speech or singing, therefore developing breath management for how and when to regulate the breathing is part of the training.

Practise it

Practise the inspired t'ai chi sequence above. Be creative with different vowel sounds and consonants. Explore which movement sequence you like best. Try them in different orders, and change the timings for each section.

Tips for teachers

Using inspiration from t'ai chi sequences allows time to develop movement with breath. Should your students be interested in developing this work further, there are websites and organizations that you will see in Appendix 2 that you could point them to. Sequences 2–4 can be repeated over and over again playing with pitch, perhaps even creating harmonies. However, always come back to a neutral laryngeal setting by finding the mid-note of the vocal range, then back to a humming sound and finally the last sequence with breath. This begins to build the stamina of breath and movement. If we consider the analogy of an athlete, the cool down from a marathon or any other sport will suggest that those individuals who run, or swim, or cycle do not stand still once the race is over, but keep moving and engaging muscles at a much lower intensity in order to reduce lactic acid build-up, aid recovery and help the heart rate return to a resting rate. This, then, is a good 'cool down' sequence as well as a good warm-up.

Feel it first

Accessing the breath (Video)

- In pairs, place your hands on your partner's lower ribs, and engage the breath by having almost an excited breath in, on the inhalation. On the exhalation release the breath on the following sounds:
  - fff, fff, fff, fff, fff.
  - sh, sh, sh.
  - vvv, vvv, vvv.

- Now try to do this on your own. Place your hands on your ribs and begin with the fff, fff, fff.
- Then try the sh, sh, sh.
- Next try the vvv, vvv, vvv.
- Now make a huvv, huvv, huvv sound.

Understand it

The ribcage holds the heart and lungs. It is attached to the thoracic spine and consists of 24 ribs. They spring from either side of the spine into two sets of 12 ribs:

7 pairs of true ribs (numbered 1 to 7, so-called because they are attached to the breastbone [sternum]);

3 pairs of false ribs (numbered 8, 9 and 10) which are attached to rib number 7 at the front;

2 pairs of floating ribs (numbered 11 and 12) attached to back of the spine but unattached at the front.

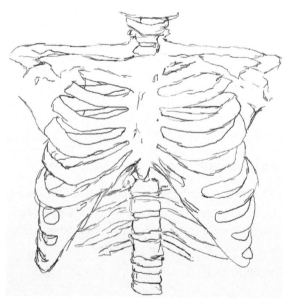

Figure 2.1 The ribcage.

Think of the ribcage much like a birdcage, in that it houses the lungs and heart. It is the muscles around this cage that make breath happen: the diaphragm and the intercostal muscles. The diaphragm is a dome-shaped sheath of muscle that is attached to the lower end of the sternum, ribs and the lungs. The lungs themselves do not create breath. Breathing in is caused by the diaphragm moving downwards and increasing the volume of the chest cavity. In turn, this lowers the air pressure in the lungs and they fill with air to equalize the air pressure. In this way inhalation causes oxygen-rich air to travel into the millions of alveoli (tiny air sacs) within the lungs. Exhalation is a reverse sequence of this; the diaphragm relaxes back into its dome shape, the chest cavity now has a smaller volume and the air pressure is higher than outside. Air then flows out of the lungs to make the pressures equal once more, carrying the body's carbon dioxide gas away through the nose or mouth.

In breath for life, the diaphragm is working constantly. However, with speech and singing your other muscles help out a great deal. The external intercostal muscles, which are attached to the outside borders of the ribs, contract and bring the ribs along for a ride, raising and expanding the ribcage and the lungs. On exhalation, while the external intercostal muscles relax, the internal intercostal muscles, which are attached to the internal borders of the ribs, help to bring everything back to rest with ease.

In dance the requirement is to let the lowest or floating ribs be as far away from the hips in order to create space. As a consequence of this, some tension may creep into the upper body such as the chest and shoulders.

Practise it

- Place your hands on your lower ribs (you can do this with a partner) and engage the ribs by an inhalation. The breath inhalation should not be audible, but it should feel like an excited sound.

- Now exhale on the following voiceless sounds:
    - fff, fff, fff, fff.
    - sh, sh, sh, sh, sh, sh.

- Release the breath on the sound of firing arrows on ft, ft, ft.
- Now exhale on the following voiced sounds:
    - vvv, vvv, vvv, vvv.
    - huvv, huvv, huvv.

Phonation – understanding the size of vocal folds

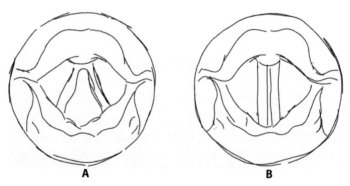

Figure 2.2 The vocal folds: with the vocal folds open (A) and closed (B).

Feel it first

- Let's begin by looking down at your feet; look at the size of them and the shape of them as you walk about the room.
- Now look at the size of your legs in relation to your feet and the energy required to move you around.
- Now look at your arms, and pick up something heavy and notice the energy required from the muscles in your shoulders, upper arms and hands.

- Next look at your hands and pick up something lighter, a book or a pen or something that requires your hands and fingers to work together. Notice the muscles that have to come together in order for the task to be achieved.

- Now look down at your hand and notice your little finger, then look at the nail on your little finger. Imagine two lines from your cuticle to the end of your nail; those two imaginary lines are roughly the size of your vocal folds. Small, aren't they? They range in size from 15 mm for the average female up to 22 mm for the average male.

Understand it

The process of phonation or voicing as it is known, is created when the vocal folds, which are inside the larynx, vibrate. For this to happen, various forces need to come into play. First, air needs to be exhaled from the lungs. As the escaping air reaches the glottis (the space between the vocal folds), laryngeal muscles work to bring the vocal folds together (adduction). Air pressure then builds up beneath the adducted folds until they are blown apart. When the air pressure drops across the glottis again, the folds come back together until the whole cycle repeats itself making what is sometimes known as a clear or clean sound. For sustained vocalization, this process happens hundreds of times a second. The vocal folds therefore need the support and management of breath in order for them to come together and then blow apart to vibrate and make sound. In whispering, an unvoiced form of phonation, the vocal folds are only slightly adducted and therefore cannot vibrate; however, the breath passes between the folds creating an audible sound of modified speech. These sounds are airy, and can sound mysterious, sensual or even sinister.

Practise it

- Now quietly speak the text below; it is part of the second chorus from *Henry V*.

Now all the youth of England are on fire,
And silken dalliance in the wardrobe lies.
Now thrive the armourers, and honour's thought
Reigns solely in the breast of every man.
They sell the pasture now to buy the horse,
Following the mirror of all Christian kings
With wingèd heels, as English Mercurys.
For now sits Expectation in the air
And hides a sword, from hilts unto the point,
With crowns imperial, crowns and coronets
Promised to Harry and his followers.
The French, advised by good intelligence
Of this most dreadful preparation,
Shake in their fear, and with pale policy
Seek to divert the English purposes.

What can you feel?

Can you feel the movement of the ribs opening out?

Or lifting upwards?

What happens when you exhale?

Does the ribcage move down and in?

Can you feel the intercostal muscles working?

Can you feel the muscles as they begin to cover your fingers as they relax?

Tips for teachers

When thinking about rib expansion, the ribs should expand
on an inhalation with the breath entering the mouth, like a
surprised gasp of air. The ribs should feel lifted and large,
allowing the back muscles to engage. To feel this further
you could raise a chair above the head and breathe in and
out, feeling the expansion. I prefer to think of an image

such as angel wings attached to the back and these wings are an extension of your upper arms and back. This angel, then, is swimming through syrup. I feel this activates the back muscles and raises the ribs more effectively and consciously engages the creative mind. However, be mindful to keep the shoulders down and relaxed.

The sounds like the /v/ and /f/ etc. stop too much air flowing through and escaping; the vvvv sound in particular allows the air to be trapped and helps regulate the air pressure. Accessing the breath in this way allows you to feel the rib expansion and the effort for the breath sequence, creating awareness in the movement of the ribs.

These exercises are for feeling the ribs activate, and are also a wonderful way to explore the beginning of accessing the breath. Try the same exercise of feeling the activation of the ribs on a variety of sounds, keeping all the sounds voiceless. Images work very well, but perhaps ask the students to choose their own image; you may find that works better for them.

Practise it further

- In pairs, one student (a) stands behind the other student (b), placing their hands on their partner's ribcage.

- Student (b) breathes in and out trying to expand the ribs and push their partner's hands away; breathe in and out to your own pace. Notice if the shoulders want to rise up on every inhalation.

- Remind yourself that you are isolating the ribcage.

- As you breathe in imagine you are counting on the in-breath to 5. Then slowly release to the count of 5.

- Try to increase the count on the in-breath and then slowly release on the count out. As you gain in confidence on this isolation, increase the count to 10 or 15 both in and out.

- Change partner position and repeat the exercise.
- Place your hands on your own ribcage and try the following sounds:
  - sss, sss, sss, sss, sss.
  - sh, sh, sh, sh, sh, sh, sh, sh, sh, sh, sh, sh.
  - kkk, kkk, kkk, kkk, kkk.
  - ttt, ttt, ttt, ttt, ttt, ttt.
  - ppp, ppp, ppp, ppp, ppp.
  - fff, fff, fff, fff, fff, fff, fff.

How do you feel?

What is it like to notice something you have been naturally doing your whole life?

Can you see your breath in terms of colours, numbers or waves?

Perhaps you have your own image?

Can you imagine the breath leaving your body and then coming back to it?

How do you imagine your breath?

Does it feel like an ocean wave, much like the tide?

The diaphragm and breath

Feel it first

Lie down and feel it.

- Lie on the floor in semi-supine, and either imagine your belly rising and falling much like a balloon or place a shoe or book on your tummy. Take a nice deep breath in and notice how the tummy rises to the ceiling. Imagine the balloon enlarging with your breath and then slowly decreasing in size as your tummy rises and falls.
- Now breathe out, allowing the tummy to fall back towards your spine.

Figure 2.3 Inflated and deflated balloons.

How does it feel to have the object on your tummy?

Can you see the object rise and fall?

Does this give you a greater understanding of the rise and fall of breath in the body?

Well done! You are engaging your diaphragm to move up and down as you breathe in and out. You have also isolated your chest breathing, your rib breathing and your abdominal breathing. We shall look at them all now in greater depth.

- Stay lying on the floor with both legs outstretched, then bend one leg at the knee and hold it towards your chest with your hands clasped around it. Stretch out the other leg. Mark the beginning of the pose with an exhalation. In yoga this is known as *wind pose*.

- As you breathe in and out, feel the harmony you create with your body, as you bring your knee closer to your chest, and the physical connection to your tummy and your back to the floor.

- When you have spent 1 minute in this position breathing in and out, change legs.
- Then repeat the exercise, humming. Repeat on both sides.
- When both sides are completed, release the legs and have a full body stretch allowing a sigh to escape from your mouth.
- Keep the jaw nice and relaxed and release the sound further.

Understand it

This pose is known as the wind pose in Yin Yoga and allows the deep fascia of the hip and groin to be released. It also, it is said, aids the digestive system, which sits below the diaphragm, allowing blood to flow to the colon. Breathing in and out in a held position, for up to 3 minutes, allows time for the body to adjust, to deepen the pose, to feel connected to the floor and to feel the length of breath, in harmony with your body. As your lower stomach comes into contact with your thigh, you are able to feel the movement of your breath more keenly.

In order to make sound for speech (phonation), the power source (breath) comes from the lungs with help from the chest, back and abdominal muscles, when we have allowed the diaphragm to release.

When we expand our ribs, on an in-breath, they swing, rise and move into action, which happens in harmony with the diaphragm, as it expands towards our ribs too. If the abdominal muscles are released and relaxed down and out, this allows the diaphragm to drop in a downwards motion, and the lower lungs move with it. On every in-breath (inhalation) as the diaphragm flattens and moves in a downward motion, the lungs will increase in overall size (Fig. 2.4A).

On every outward breath (exhalation), the abdominals (which are made up of various muscles including the oblique muscles,

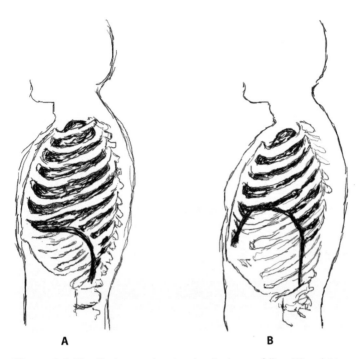

A   B

Figure 2.4 The diaphragm: showing the diaphragm falling (A) and rising (B) on the inhalation and exhalation.

the transverse muscles, and rectus abdominis muscles) bind the abdomen, pushing the stomach contents inwards and upwards and thus helping the diaphragm move upwards (Fig. 2.4B). The resulting pressure change in the lungs means that air can be expelled for speech and song.

When we move less, or we are resting, we only use about 15 per cent of our lungs' vital capacity. This is known as passive breathing, and uses on average half a litre of air. However, the average total lung capacity from maximum breath in and out in an adult male is 6 litres. The more exertion needed for physical activity or vocal performance such as dancing, singing and speaking requires the respiratory system to work much harder. We have evolved to speak, sing and dance and this requires the lungs to expand to a greater extent than for passive breathing.

When we breathe for a run, a jog or a skip, we generally exhale on alternate legs. This is known as rhythmic breathing, where it is possible to coordinate the breath with action. Inhaling to lift a leg and exhaling to drop the leg in the run, skip or jog, allows for both sides of the body to breathe equally. As someone who participates in swimathons, I am used to rhythmically breathing bilaterally, or every other side, allowing for both synergy and symmetry across the body, and increasing efficiency. Therefore it is possible to access the correct breath for the task by taking sips of breath for singing and speaking when also moving, and to use the correct amount of breath to utilize the movement of muscles.

Practise it

- Continue to lie in semi-supine and close your eyes.

- Place your hand on your collar bone (clavicle) or your partner's, and notice your breath as you breathe in through the nose and out through the mouth, inhaling and exhaling. Try to imagine your shoulders as relaxed as possible, so that only the tiniest movement from the chest and sternum rises and falls on the in- and out-breath.

- Now place the hands on your lower ribs just above the waist and again breathe in and breathe out. Notice how the ribs expand on the in-breath and collapse on the out-breath.

- Try this again so that the ribs are slowly managed in an upward or outward movement on the in-breath and a downward or backward movement on the out-breath.

- Now place your hand on your lower tummy area, and breathe in and breathe out.

- Notice that on the 'in-breath' your tummy falls into your hand and on the 'out-breath' your tummy moves back towards your spine.

- Try the exercises again standing in neutral and see if you can feel the space or time between the in-breath and the out-breath.

In order to feel a deeper connection to your breath, it is possible to utilize one nostril at a time, closing over the other nostril. This is known as 'prana' breathing.

Feel it first

Prana breathing in sitting position.

- Sit on a chair or sit crossed-legged on the floor.
- Place your first two fingers in the middle of your forehead.
- Now place your thumb against the right nostril and breathe in through your left nostril.
- Now place your ring finger against the left nostril and breathe out through your right nostril.
- Alternate between closing off one nostril and breathing in and out of one nostril then change sides. Try these exercises for 3 minutes.

Understand it

Breath is known in some cultures as the 'prana' or the 'chi', or the 'life-force'. Connecting with your breath for speech while engaging the thought process allows a deeper connection to your voice, power, status, pitch range, movement, sound and intention. Deep breath management can release tension, create a calming effect, be meditative and can give you, the performer, control of your nerves, creating harmony in the body and control of your sound. Prana breathing works on harmonizing your breath and connecting with the left and right brain. It is thought that this kind of breathing awakens and activates brainwaves, and through stimulation of this unique breathing, we can engage with creativity, energy and a sense of grounding.

We often mistakenly hold our breath in standing poses or dance positions. Through some of this deep breath work, movement has a greater release and therefore you may be able to passively stretch into poses more effectively and efficiently. This breath work will also aid connection to the movement of Rudolf Laban, and other forms of creative movement, choreography and dance, making you aware of breath management, harmony of thought, breath and body.

Practise it

- Continue to sit on a chair and practise the breathing in and out; this time imagine a colour entering one nostril, and leaving the other nostril as you continue with the prana breathing.

- Explore breathing in and out differing colours.

- Perhaps allow a musical note to enter the nostril and then out of the other nostril.

- Next, stand up in neutral and begin with a solid connection to the floor. It is this connection which is often called 'getting grounded'. It allows us to feel our bodies taking stock of what is around us from the feet up, and creates firm foundations much like those of a building.

- Breathe in and out, and feel the stability without rigidity. This stability allows us to simply breathe and feel connected to the ground, and feeling grounded allows time for the body to settle, and to release any chatter that may be going on in our heads, listening to our bodies without judgement or comment. This stillness and silence brings a heightened sense of connectedness and grounding.

- Keep your eyes open and breathe in and out.

What do you feel?

Can you feel the breath enter your ribs, abdominal area and chest?

Can you feel the movement of your body as it takes a breath in and out?

Practise it further

Blow it out.

- Sitting upright on a chair, take a leaf, feather, paper page or other light object like a tissue and blow it; try a soft sustained breath, as if you are keeping the object moving gently with your breath.

- Still using the tissue, try a much more forceful or faster breath on exhalation to the sound shhhh, shhhh, as if shooing away a cat.

- Blow on each finger and notice the tummy rise and fall.

- Now try a rhythmic breath on sharp blasts of air using the sound fff, fff, fff, fff.

- Take a feather, leaf or tissue and hold it in front of your mouth and speak some text.

How much does the feather, leaf or tissue move?

How hard is your breath working to move it back and forth?

How conscious were you of your in-breath?

Did you think about your breath?

Share a breath and breathe.

In pairs:

- Stand opposite your partner and try breathing together; share a breath and breathe.

- Change partners and again breathe in and out whilst observing them. They in turn will be doing the same with you. The harmony of breathing together creates a rapport.

- Now try and match each other's breath patterns, as this further enhances rapport and relieves tension, creates harmony and establishes a common vibration.

- Try different emotional states such as happy, sad, agitated, angry, and notice the breathing of yourself and your partner.

- Try breathing in pairs, where one of you is in a heightened emotional state (perhaps try anger) and one of you is in a calm state.

Are you able to affect the breathing of your partner?

Have you become affected by their breath patterns?

What do you feel?

What do you notice in your partner in each of these states of emotion?

How can you use breath to calm someone down?

Laugh it off.

- Bring this breath work into laughing with your partner.

- Start by standing opposite them and look them in the eyes and begin to create a harmonious sense of joy, first by smiling and then through to laughter. This further engages the diaphragm and takes away any tension or seriousness that may have encroached on the work, by laughing it out and laughing it off.

- Now begin to bring your breath under some management; breathe in through the nose and out through the mouth.

- Finally get yourself grounded and centred again.

Gym breath into speech and song

The amount of breath required for any task is essential. Therefore let us explore the breath management and effort required for the tasks set below.

Feel it first

Increasing exercise tolerance for extended breath capacity.

- Begin by standing in neutral, arms by the side, long torso and long neck.

- Place your hands on your shoulder and circle your arms 10 times one way and then 10 times the other way.

- Now speak aloud by counting from 1 to 10.

  What do you notice about your breathing?

- Now standing on one leg, swing the other leg from side to side or forward and backward 10 times, then swap legs.

- Now speak aloud by counting from 1 to 20.

  What has changed about your breathing?

  Are you breathing in through the nose and out through the mouth?

- Now try and lift something above your head (it could be a book, a block or a chair), keeping your shoulders down.

- Begin by speaking some text or counting aloud. Try this for 2 minutes. Put down the object you have been holding and speak the text again.

- Now begin to walk around the studio/room, slowly at first then become faster and faster even though you are still walking. Do this for 1 minute then stop and say the alphabet.

  Has your breathing changed?

- Now jog around the room for 2 minutes, then stop and speak a line of text.

  What do you notice about your breathing?

- Using a skipping rope, skip for 3 minutes, then stop and sing a song or speak sing a poem.

  What do you notice about your breathing?

Understand it

In the exercise above, you will have explored your active breathing, the breath capacity and how it feels differently in movement than it did in stillness. You will have noticed your ribs expanding for breath, and your chest breathing was more engaged as a short intake of breath for each physical movement was necessary. You may have noticed the abdomen moving in and out. You will notice your breath capacity expands for the task required. It is thought that you cannot increase your lung capacity, as your physiology is what it is; however, I would argue that it is possible to increase the *sense of* capacity due to exercise tolerance, dance being a major contributor in this case. With frequent exercise, it is possible to increase the capacity between 5 and 15 per cent. That is different from saying the size of your lungs will increase.

The sequence above is often practised the first time you enter a gym with a personal trainer. The gym instructor is ascertaining your breathing whilst asking you a series of questions, noticing your breath recovery time.

Were you aware of your abdominals engaging?

Did you realize that in order to do the task you had to breathe in through the mouth rather than the nose?

An example of this kind of gym breathing is used in the musical *Legally Blonde* and asks the character Brooke Taylor-Windham to dance and skip with a skipping rope for over 3 minutes whilst singing the song 'I'll have you whipped into shape' as the character she is portraying is an aerobics instructor. Then immediately after the song and dance sequence is over, the character speaks without appearing out of breath. This gym breath training requires practice on a regular basis.

Practise it

Try holding a conversation whilst running or jogging or skipping. Build your stamina up slowly by doing the exercise below whilst talking.

- Walk and talk for 1 minute.
- Jog and talk for 1 minute.
- Run and talk for 1 minute.

Now to cool down do the reverse.

- Run and talk for 1 minute.
- Jog and walk for 1 minute.
- Walk and talk for 1 minute.
- Stand still and notice your breathing.
- Try holding a conversation whilst running or jogging or skipping.

How do you feel? How hard are you breathing?

Can you talk or is your breathing affecting the quality of speech?

Tips for teachers

Try to get the students to walk and talk, having a conversation, then after 2 minutes stop the exercise. The students can continue to speak. Ask them to notice their breath capacity, noticing how hard it is to speak.

Get them to repeat the exercises with variations such as jogging then singing, skipping then singing or speaking.

Dance, voice and movement

Tap dancing

Feel it first

Increasing tolerance.

- Try tap dancing, perhaps a sequence you know well, and keep the sequence going for 3 minutes.
- Now try the same routine again, this time counting aloud or saying the alphabet.
- Now tap the same sequence again, this time speaking some lines of text or a poem, each time keep it going for 3 minutes.
- Now tap the sequence for the last time, only now you must sing a song. Perhaps the song '42nd Street', from the musical *42nd Street*.
- Now stop and try speaking a line of text.

How is your breathing?

How does the dancing affect the song?

Is your mouth dry?

Movement and breath: Laban Efforts

Explore the use of your breath in movement feeling how connection to breath helps the movement qualities of the 'Laban Efforts' listed below.

Feel it first

Using just your arms at first, explore the Laban Efforts.

- Slash your arms about and feel your breath. Then slash your arms and vocalize a sound.

- Now try dabbing your arms or fingers and feel your breath, then try dabbing and vocalize a sound.

- Now try wringing your hands and notice your breath, then wring your arms or hands and vocalize a sound.

- Now flick your arms, hands or fingers and notice your breath and then flick and vocalize a sound.

- Try gliding your arms in the space and notice your breath and then glide whilst vocalizing a sound.

- Now try pressing your hands as if they have resistance and notice your breath, then try pressing and vocalize sound.

- Now try floating around the room, where possible just engaging your arms, noticing your breath, and then vocalizing a sound.

- Finally punch the air and notice your breath and try punching the air and vocalize a sound.

How did that feel?

What is your body feeling?

What is your voice feeling?

What is your breath doing?

Which of these efforts did you enjoy the most?

What sound or breath inspired or challenged you?

What do you feel about your body and voice in the space?

Understand it

The movement work of Rudolf Laban is a form of dance that takes into consideration the personality and potential of the dancer. He was a choreographer, dancer and movement specialist who created physical efforts that describe movement.

Therefore it is not a learnt set of sequences alone, but relies on the MTP to observe with attention to detail why and how a character moves across the space: the basic questions an actor asks, of what and why and how. The rhythms and spaces of time are considered, and the breath effort associated with each movement.

Rudolf Laban's Eight Efforts of floating, dabbing, wringing, thrusting, pressing, flicking, slashing and gliding, combined with the three energies of weight, space and time, developed a practice widely used by many conservatoires to engage the actor's understanding of how a character moves and the energy and effort required. Using the Laban Efforts allows the MTP to explore movement and voice together.

Practise it

Explore the eight Efforts, using the rest of the body, perhaps just the legs, engaging the breath in a physical state and a resting state, each of these done with some text. Perhaps a poem or a sonnet. Perhaps a poem in another accent.

- Try *floating* around the room, using text.
- Try the *wringing* effort with your hands together, using text.
- Try the *thrusting* effort with your hands in the air, using text.
- Next try the efforts *pressing, flicking, slashing, gliding* and *dabbing*, all using text.

With each of these Efforts you will have noticed an emotional connection, some of them you may enjoy and some not so much. Continue to develop your body in space as you explore the efforts with sound.

What have you noticed about your breath in each of these efforts?

Does the work feel internal or external?

How does it feel to communicate with text?

Does it affect the Laban Effort?

Does it reduce its intensity?

Feeling the breath of a quiet voice

Feel it first

- In pairs, whisper (or speak very quietly) in your partner's ear some text, perhaps use the text of a song, poem or sonnet.
- Whisper or speak very quietly something happy.
- Next whisper or speak very quietly something sad.
- Finally whisper or speak very quietly something creepy.

How does it feel to speak like this?

What mood is created?

How does it feel to have someone whisper in your ear?

Ticklish? Creepy?

Understand it

When we whisper, it is an unvoiced form of phonating sound where the vocal folds do not fully adduct, causing air or breath to pass between the arytenoid cartilages, creating an unsteady turbulence of air during speech. This can tire the vocal folds if done for too long; however, for short exercises it is possible to create a feeling for both participant and listener – there can be wonderful ambience, or a range of emotions.

Tips for teachers

A great exercise taught to me as part of a workshop with Cicely Berry, and I believe further enhanced by David Carey, was to look at the first scene of William Shakespeare's *Hamlet*. Have the students in groups talking quietly or whispering, imagining someone is listening in, like the enemy or like the ghost himself. This creates tension and atmosphere, and is a great way to introduce the first scene of a play. Perhaps have a student walking up and down so that the students in the scene can only speak when that person is out of range.

What do the observers notice? Has tension been created?

Practise it

- Using the text below speak into your hand while cupping your ear with the other hand so that the hand around the ear acts like a speaker.

    Remember me when I am gone away,
    Gone far away into the silent land;
    When you can no more hold me by the hand.
    Nor I half turn to go yet turning stay,
    Remember me when no more day by day,
    You tell me of our future that you plann'd.

- Check in with your voice every now and then, by completing a vocal check.

    Vocal check list:

- Whimper like dog.
- Meow like cat.
- Gently siren up and down the scale.
- Gently hum up and down the scale.

The volume levels should be low: if 10 were the loudest on a volume scale then the sound check should be around 3 or 4. This is a great way of clarifying your own voice journey, and your voice will give you instant feedback, both in sound and how it feels. When you are listening to your body and voice it will be your instant feedback and allow you to take responsibility for the sounds you make.

Breath and core strength

How does the instruction 'pull up, hold in and lengthen' in a dance class work in conjunction with the instruction in a voice class of 'release, allow, let go', and make any sense in relation to breath management? Well, of course it is impossible, it is a contradiction. The MTP needs to be able to understand these differences. Tension and relaxation through breath work is one way; allowing a release of the stomach muscles of the abdominals and stretching the core muscles in an exercise such as sphinx works well. Core strength is welcome in a voice class and core muscles should be engaged, even for spine rolls. However, *engagement* means just that, not forced or held as this can cause problems for the diaphragm. The exercises below are essentially about engaging with core strength whilst in harmony with breath management.

Feel it first

Activation of core strength and breath.

- Re-engage with the neutrals: N–, neutral and N+; and feel the energy difference between all three.

- Stand in neutral and be aware of your top line.
- Now stand in N–, and be aware of your top line.
- Now stand in N+, and be aware of your top line.
- Imagine you have a very long neck and your shoulders travelling in a downwards motion.
- The pelvis should be relaxed in a downward motion, gently activating the tummy button to move towards the spine. The abdominals should still remain flat when engaged, a flat muscle rather than bunched muscle, which is a good way of knowing you are working your core strength correctly. When done correctly, this helps with lower-back issues and aids posture, allowing you to move more freely and adopt a secure body balance.
- Place your thumb into your tummy button and fan out the rest of your fingers so that the little finger touches the top of your lower tummy or pubis bone. Now imagine a gold thread pulling its way towards your spine at 100 per cent of engagement, as you reel in your tummy towards your spine.
- Now release to 50 per cent of that core engagement.
- Play with the three stages of complete relaxation of the tummy flop, to total core engagement at 100 per cent and then find the middle ground, which is 50 per cent core activity.
- Now count aloud numbers 1 to 10 as in 1; 1, 2; 1, 2, 3; 1, 2, 3, 4; 1, 2, 3, 4, 5; and so on. As you engage in this activity, pull the imaginary gold thread attached to your tummy button towards your spine.
- Now lie in semi-supine and repeat the exercises above.

How does it feel to activate the core at 100 per cent then dropping to 50 per cent?

Understand it

Imagine that, for an Olympic athlete to activate total core strength, they must employ up to 100 per cent engagement of abdominal muscles, which are moving back towards the spine (such as for a sit up). Although this level of activation would be necessary in much of dance training, in voice training I would suggest 50 per cent engagement of core strength, and minimal engagement of the oblique muscles (or the side muscles) – perhaps as little as 20 per cent. This means that the core muscles are still activated but will not compromise the intake of breath or activate the ribs (although they are attached), and will ensure the diaphragm can still move freely. Core strength also stabilizes the lower back for good posture.

The abdominal muscles are engaged at all times in dance as if the tummy button is being gently pulled via a gold thread trying to hook onto the inside of the spine. (This is a lovely image from the dance teacher Rachael Kerridge.) The engagement of stomach muscles are then only activated below the tummy button. You will notice that with a drop of 50 per cent core activation, the oblique muscles are less engaged, allowing you to manage your breath support, and further allowing the diaphragm to drop downwards on the exhalation and release upwards on the inhalation (the natural movement of the diaphragm). The transverse muscle, whilst toned and activated, can also still be released.

Practise it

Activation of core strength and speech.

- Stand on one leg and say the alphabet with 100 per cent core strength.
- Now repeat the exercise with 50 per cent core strength.
- Change legs and speak the months of the year with 100 per cent core strength.

- Then again with 50 per cent core strength.

- Change legs again, raise the arms above the head and speak a poem with 100 per cent core strength. Then repeat with 50 per cent core strength.

- Change legs again and raise the arms above the head and bend the supporting leg using 100 per cent core strength. Now try the same again using 50 per cent core strength.

What do you feel after the 100 per cent core strength exercise?

Are you able to establish a clear sound with good breath support with the 50 per cent of core strength?

Buttocks

Feel it first

Releasing tension of thighs and buttocks using breath.

- Sitting on a chair with your feet flat on the floor, tense each thigh separately and together. Note how your bottom will also engage; note if you are holding your breath. Mark the hold of each buttock with an inhalation and relax on an exhalation.

- Sitting on the floor, use a prickle ball, tennis ball or something similar to press your thigh against, and mark the pose with an exhalation. Use the breath to release any buttock or thigh tension.

- Staying on the floor, feel the muscles softening and melting into the ball. Mark the pose with an exhalation. This is a wonderful way to explore and massage any thigh tension, and feel it release.

- Standing up against a wall, place the ball against your buttocks, thighs or shoulders. Whilst you are leaning against the wall, the ball is between you and the wall; this will massage out any tension you may have. Mark the pose with an exhalation.

Understand it

Dancers often experience tension in their thighs and bottoms due to the level of dance training, which many will have been doing since four years of age. The muscles in the thighs should feel long and strong with a sense of support, structure and foundation to the rest of the body. They should not be relaxed, but active. This does not mean tense, it means they are engaged and activated or fired up. I have often noticed that dancers who are asked to stand with their feet parallel in a voice class often engage muscles such as the gluteus maximus and the thighs, with the knees becoming locked, normally in anticipation of dancing. In fact most dancers find it hard to switch off their muscles long enough to relax.

Practise it

Play some music, maybe from a musical, and move your thighs and bottom to this music. At all times be mindful of your breath. Allow the voluntary breathing associated with minimal exercise.

Are you trying to hold your breath?

Can you see how your gluteus maximus (bottom) wants to engage when the thighs are working?

Suggested songs

Here are some suitable songs for you to try:

'I'll Have You Whipped Into Shape' from the musical *Legally Blonde* by Laurence O'Keefe and Nell Benjamin (2007).
'Anything Goes' from the musical *Anything Goes* by Cole Porter (1934).
'You Can't Stop the Beat' from the musical *Hairspray* by Marc Shaiman and Scott Wittman (2002).

'Chorus Line' from the musical *A Chorus line*, music by Marvin Hamlisch, lyrics by Edward Kleban and book by James Kirkwood Jr. and Nicholas Dante (1975).

Suggested texts

Here are some suitable texts for you to try:

W. H. Auden, 'Stop the Clocks'
Mary Elizabeth Frye, 'Do Not Stand at My Grave and Weep'
Gerard Manley Hopkins, 'Earnest, Earthless, Equal, Attuneable'
Rudyard Kipling, 'If'
Christina Rossetti, 'Remember'
Percy Bysshe Shelley, 'Music, When Soft Voices Die'

Further reading

BBC (2004), *The Nation's Favourite Poems*, London: BBC Worldwide Ltd.

Bloom, K. and R. Shreeves (1998), *Moves*, London: Routledge.

Boston, J. and R. Cook (2009), *Breath in Action*, London: Jessica Kingsley Publishers.

Brizendine, L. (2007), *The Female Brain*, New York: Bantam Books.

Cook, O. (2008), *Singing with Your Own Voice*, London: Nick Hern Books.

Cook, R. (2012), *Voice and the Young Actor*, London: Methuen.

Franklin, E. (2004), *Conditioning for Dance*, Leeds: Human Kinetics.

Melton, J. with K. Tom (2012), *One Voice*, 2nd edn, Illinois: Waveland Press.

Newlove, J. (1993), *Laban for Actors and Dancers*, London: Nick Hern Books.

Rodgers, J., ed. (2002), *The Complete Voice and Speech Workout*, Montclair, NJ: Applause.

Stark, J. (2008), *Bel Canto a History of Vocal Pedagogy*, University of Toronto Press.

3 Building the Voice

Keywords: placement, vowels, intoning, imagination, impulse, creativity

The deep song of joy and pain is primitive and known to many.
SPANISH GITANO PROVERB

Introduction

What is meant by building the voice? Isn't our voice already built? What do voice and singing teachers mean by this? Perhaps they mean 'can I improve my vocal power or strength?' Sometimes these statements are meant to explain and explore resonance, timbre, tone and power of the voice. However, building the voice is much more than this. The voice is 'built' by engaging the body, understanding a clear recognition of relaxation and tension, the engagement of your breath management, and secure posture and alignment. And all through the prism of emotional engagement through actor training, capitalizing on this, to secure a healthy voice, for longevity of a performing career. Being technically accomplished alone does not necessarily mean a *great* triple threat performer. In this chapter, we build on the blocks of previous chapters of posture and breath to explore the beating heart of building a voice through the emotional connection to what is being said and why. The expression of voice, the dynamic responses and depth of feelings are explored by linking thoughts with voice, breath and into text. We explore how vowels are especially significant in establishing an emotional connection.

Take, for example, Imelda Staunton's performance of Mama Rose in *Gypsy* by Stephen Sondheim at London's Savoy Theatre in 2016, where she won an Olivier award for Best Actress in a Musical. If one were listening to her technical abilities as a singer alone, we would say she is a creative accomplished singer; however, it is the heart and soul that Staunton brings to every performance, requiring emotions of such a heightened level from speech to shouting to screaming to singing, that brings the pain and suffering of the character to the role. Her performance is built upon her foundations as an actress, her impulse and imagination, the depth of her emotional engagement, and the creativity she has brought to that role.

Vowels

Emotions in words are created, it is thought, through the vowel and the vowel sounds. Consonants give the word its sense, therefore the power of the vowel sound is integral to building the voice. Shakespeare's use of vowels is evident in many of his plays using the 'O' and 'AH' sounds for emotional effect, and many poets use the length of vowels to give depth and meaning to a phrase or to allow the weight of emotion to land, so that the weight of the word feels strong and powerful, and tugs at our heart.

Feel it first

Long vowels with rock and roll (Video)

- Begin by standing in neutral, then reminding yourself of the posture checklist for both the other neutrals, the neutral plus (N+) and neutral minus (N–). Remember to always activate (N+) by the use of the image of the angel swimming through syrup; this set-up will help the engagement of the back muscles and a natural opening of the chest, without force or tension, and remember for N– to feel the energy in the balls of your feet, keeping your shoulders down and back. Think of your top line. Allow yourself to explore all three poses whilst engaging in the exercises below.

Reminder of neutral plus (N+).

- Now stand in N+, begin with legs in an open stance, knees slightly bent, with space between hips and lowest rib.
- Feel you have a long torso, a long neck, and your chin is resting on your four fingers, with the thumb resting on the chest, creating a large C.
- Your weight ratio roughly 55 per cent at the back of the foot and 45 per cent at the front of the foot.

Rocking back. Centre yourself in neutral after each exercise.

- Rock back and say OO as in spoon.
- Now rock back and say AW as in paw.
- Next, rock back and say AH as in car.
- Then rock back and say EYE as in pie.
- Next, rock back and say AYE as in pay.
- Finally rock back and say EE as in please.
- Repeat all the above, this time intoning the sounds.

What do you feel about the rock and roll back and forth?

Are you able to feel the engagement of the back muscles?

Short vowels with rock and roll. In N– create the sounds listed below exploring the shortness of the vowels. Centre yourself in neutral after each exercise.

- Roll forward and say I as in hit.
- Next roll forward and say E as in pet.
- Then roll forward and say A as in cat.

- Next roll forward and say O as in hot.
- Finally roll forward and say U as in put.
- Repeat all the above, this time intoning the sounds.

Tips for teachers

You could explore this further with both the posture and the long and short vowels. Play with the sequence by starting in neutral, then rock back for the long vowels into N+ then roll forward into N− to create a short vowel sound. This helps give physical embodiment to the length of a vowel.

You can decide on which long and short vowels to use and in what sequence.

Understand it

Physically engaging with the length of a vowel can help create a sense of feeling, power and creativity, which is not governed by the music of a song.

I devised the rock and roll method having explored the various types of neutral that is understood by each discipline of voice, singing and dance. The rock and roll method allows you to feel the length of the vowel, by engaging each of the neutrals for each discipline the MTP encounters. Allowing the impulse of the rock and roll to engage with the weight of the vowels improves the perception of its length, its weight, its impulse and its meaning.

It becomes a physical and visual representation of the vowel length itself. Feeling the rock and roll method kinaesthetically helps the length of vowel enter the body, allowing a deeper connection to the words, as the words become physical.

Rocking backwards and rolling forwards allows you to feel N– in the forward position, neutral in the central position and N+ in the rock back position. The shift of weight affects the muscles of legs and back and the energy and impulse used which therefore activates the correct muscle group for the task. This also gives a greater appreciation of long and short vowels.

Practise it

Now let's put these movements together to form a sequence. You can list any vowel sound that is long in length with N+, and pair it up with any short vowel with N–.

For example:

- Roll forward for A as in cat rock back to AH as in car.
- Roll forward for I as in hit, then rock back to OO as in spoon.
- Roll forward for E as in pet, then rock back to AW as in paw.
- Roll forward for UH as in butt, then rock back to EE as in please.
- Roll forward for O as in pot, then rock back to AYE as in pay.

Always allow the rocking and rolling back and forth from short vowel to long vowel.

Tips for teachers

Perhaps get the students to work on a Shakespeare sonnet. The students can all use the same sonnet taking a line each, or work on their own. Make decisions on where you would like to rock back and roll forward, or even let the students decide, and notice how this exercise affects the use of words, the joy of exploring the length of a vowel. Possibly allow the students to create their own sonnet or explore a song; this may help with the length of phrase, note or moment in a song.

Placement of sound

What do voice and singing teachers mean by placement of sound? What does forward placement mean? The placement of your voice suggests the need to focus sounds towards an area of your body or place, which you can feel, such as the chest or back for example. It is possible through breath management, activation of back muscles and intoning, to place or feel the sound in the area you wish. The sounds created, being secondary vibrations, can be felt in areas of the body such as the chest, back of the neck and the forehead.

There are many areas of the body that help focus the sound using imagery and which are more sympathetic to respond as amplifiers for sending the sound forward. The shape of the mouth, the height of the tongue, the position of the larynx, and posture all play a part in placing the voice. Think about different accents: you will notice that they all have different places where the sound is made and where the sound is placed in the mouth, including the length of the vowels. *Is the sound placed at the back of the mouth, the middle of the mouth, the front of the mouth? Does it have a twang-like quality to it?*

Feel it first

- To begin with let us start by placing the sound in different parts of the body with a hum. Build that hum so that the sound stays focused first of all around our nasal area.

- Then move the sound to your forehead, your back and chest, around your wrists, the hips and around each leg, and imagine these as being rings of light.

- Allow these rings of sound to stay close to you, perhaps on level 2 or 3 in volume terms where 10 is the loudest; perhaps this ring of sound has a little light close to you. This is the sphere of *The self.*

- Continue to hum then make a sound such as the AH as in car, but keep the sound close to you. Consider this to be these inner rings, your own inner rings of sound and light as you explore the sounds building, still keeping to *The self.*

- Now explore the sound and light you have created to allow a small group of people to hear your sound. The is the sphere of *At arm's length.*

- Next extend the sound to fill the room, imagining the rings of light from each part of your body are now filling the room. This the sphere of *To the world.*

How do you feel? Can you imagine the rings of light on each part of your body?

Did you feel them extend further out and beyond the room?

How did you find the perimeters of the rings?

How did each one affect the sound you made?

Practise it

Using the same principles of the rings of light around your body speak in the three ring perimeters: using the principles of talking to yourself, to one or two people and then to the rest of the room – *The self, At arm's length* and *To the world.*

- Place the sound using the vowel sound AH as in car, then change the shape of your mouth. *How does this affect the vowel sound?*

- Next try the EE vowel and change the shape of the mouth, at all times intoning the sound as a long vowel on one note.

- Now explore the OO vowel and change the shape of the mouth, at all times intoning the sound on one note.

You may notice that the note appears to change in pitch with the shape of the mouth.

Practise it further

- Try the sentences below from plays and musicals, using all three rings of light – *The self*, *At arm's length* and *To the world*.

  'To be or not to be, that is the question.' *Hamlet,* William Shakespeare.

  'Nobody puts baby in the corner.' *Dirty Dancing: The Musical* (2004), John Morris and Erich Bulling.

  'I'm mad as hell and I'm not gonna take it anymore.' *Network* (2017), Paddy Chayefsky.

  'I smell children.' *Mary Poppins* (1964), Sherman Brothers.

  'Maggie, we're through with lies and liars in this house. Lock the door.' *Cat on a Hot Tin Roof* (1955), Tennessee Williams.

  'You can't stop my happiness, because I like the way I am.' *Hairspray* (2007).

- Now try the chorus speech from *Henry V* Act 3 using all three stages, of *The self*, *At arm's length* and *To the world*.

  Thus with imagined wing our swift scene flies
  In motion of no less celerity
  Than that of thought. Suppose that you have seen
  The well-appointed king at Hampton pier
  Embark his royalty, and his brave fleet
  With silken streamers the young Phoebus fanning.

Play with your fancies and in them behold,
Upon the hempen tackle, shipboys climbing.
Hear the shrill whistle, which doth order give
To sounds confused. Behold the threaden sails,
Borne with th' invisible and creeping wind,
Draw the huge bottoms through the furrowed sea,
Breasting the lofty surge. Oh, do but think
You stand upon the rivage and behold
A city on th' inconstant billows dancing,
For so appears this fleet majestical
Holding due course to Harfleur. Follow, follow!
Grapple your minds to sternage of this navy
And leave your England, as dead midnight still,
Guarded with grandsires, babies, and old women,
Either past or not arrived to pith and puissance,
For who is he whose chin is but enriched
With one appearing hair that will not follow
These culled and choice-drawn cavaliers to France?

What does it feel like to say the same line with a different ring of sound?

What did you discover about the placement of your sound in each ring of light?

How does it feel to say each of these lines in three different ways?

Tips for teachers

The sequence of rings of sound and light can be done with many different types of text. I would always explore the rings of sound first, as this sets where you want to place the sound and where your students may find the depth of their voices from the inner quieter voice to the outer voice, both needing to feel authentic.

Building the vocal set using animals, archetypes, myths and legends

Myths and legends use archetypes, such as animals, ghosts and ghouls, monsters, princesses, witches, monsters, etc., and these are very much embedded as part of actor training. The creative imagination of the actor brings the archetypes alive. Archetypes, animals, myths and legends all offer the chance to be something 'other' than sounding nice, and this offers exploratory vocal and physical work. These are wonderful ways to enhance the building of the voice. *Who knows what animal you may play in your career?* Perhaps the Lion King, or a monster or ghoul as in *The Addams Family*, *Rocky Horror Show*, *Carrie the Musical*, *The Hunchback of Notre Dame*, *Beauty and the Beast* and *Shrek*, to name a few.

Feel it first

- Begin by standing in neutral.
- Punch the air and allow breath to escape.
- Now punch the air and allow a sound to escape.
- Now say yeah, yeah, yeah, like you mean it.
- Now say it again like you don't mean it at all.
- Now say na ne nan na, almost the sound children can make when taunting each other.
- Now intone oo ee oo ee oo,
- Bleat like a sheep, and imagine you have lost your baby ewe.
- Moo like a cow.
- Meow like a cat.
- Bark like a dog.
- Tweet like a bird.
- Growl like a lion.

- Grunt like a bear.
- Now try one of the above archetypes with the three rings of sound and light explored earlier. *What does it do or say about the character?*
- Try speaking a line perhaps from a play, then one from a musical.
- Next try singing a line from a song using the three rings of sound and light.

Understand it

Building the voice from speech to song as one vocal instrument takes time, using both imagination and creativity, as well as technical knowledge. Within the confines of a one-to-one singing lesson technique, whilst very important, can *sometimes* limit playfulness; therefore, the voice exercises in class are designed to utilize playfulness, exploration and imagination, so that once you are back in a singing lesson you are able to take some aspects of discovery to the singing class. The expansion of extreme pitch can be heard, and can be playful, and can be useful when moving back to speech. Some groups of sounds that can play out in an imaginative way are ghosts and ghouls, monsters, wizards and witches, prince, princess, bear, snake, rabbit, cat and dog. These playful yet useful voice and movement archetype exercises allow you and the students to fully explore the characteristics.

Practise it

- Walk around the room and imagine you are one of the following archetypes, although at some point try and play them all. Your responses to each of them will surprise you.
- Begin by physicalizing the generalized characteristics of each archetype, then when you are comfortable, explore the sounds that you make associated with that archetype.

- Speak aloud the three sentences: 'I am alone'; 'I am here'; and 'I miss you'. Spend about 2 minutes in each of the following archetypes:
  - Bear
  - Prince
  - Princess
  - Ghoul
  - Hero
  - Witch
  - Monster.
- Now try singing a song as each of the above archetypes.

What other things do they say?

What are their movements like?

How did each state make you feel?

Which one did you prefer? Why?

Tips for teachers

The exercises above, have been adapted from a masterclass with the vocal coach Bernadette O'Brien. Creating a farmyard of animals, whilst noisy, allows the opportunity to see the creative and imaginative playful sounds and movements made by your students. I have adapted these further examples below, which were originally introduced to me by David Carey, and are a wonderful way to explore voice creatively and imaginatively. In a group, make the sounds of a series of stories without words: a ship a sea in a storm; an evening at the opera; noises of the jungle.

In two groups, you can create a scene without words; it could be a café where an accident happens outside, a night at the opera where something bad happens. There must always be a beginning to establish where they are, a middle so that we know something has gone wrong, and an end where it is resolved. The other group with their eyes closed can then guess where they are and what happened.

To play with vocal extremes within a safe environment allows the students to feel playful without judgement, without the need to get the sound right by feeling the voice through experimentation.

Intoning the sound

Feel it first

- Raise the soft palate and yawn, then feel the hard palate with your tongue. Prepare for a pre-yawn now keeping the lips pursed closed. *Do you want to yawn again?*

- Feel a stretch at the back of the mouth with another yawn as you stretch the back of the mouth but keep the lips and opening of the mouth in an O as in 'hot' shape. Arthur Lessac calls this the inverted megaphone shape.

- Keeping this shape, begin sounding the list below:
  - MA MA MA
  - MAY MAY MAY
  - ME ME ME
  - LOO LEE LOO
  - LA LAY LA LAY

Do you notice that you want to almost sing the sound?
Is there vibrato in the sound?

- Now cup your hand around your mouth as if to call someone across the room, with the mouth and lips still in the O position. Try the list below:
  - Hey
  - Ho
  - Hi
  - Hello
  - Hayli
  - Heeli
  - Hooly
  - Horly
  - Hayla
  - Hello
  - Hi
  - Ho
  - Hey.
- Now swallow and siren up and down the scale, notice how your voice feels. You should feel open at the back of your oral cavity. Perhaps your soft palate feels warm and engaged.
- Now imagine you are at the top of a mountain, and call aloud these sentences:
  - We won the football!
  - Hello over there!
  - The wall is coming down!
  - Yippee, I can finally ride my bike.
  - I ran a marathon!
  - Hello – I'm coming to you.

Understand it

You will notice that once you begin to call, the extended sound of the calling leads into an almost song-like quality. *Where does speaking end and singing begin?* That is the question, and the more students think of their speaking voice as musical as possible, sharing the sound and pitch and intoning helps define the energy in the areas between the two as this extended sound of the call becomes like song.

Practise it

- Speak the lines from the previous exercise again.
- Then speak them again in the calling quality you managed earlier.
- Extend the sound to a singing quality.
- Then back to speech.

Tips for teachers

You could get your students to come up with their own sentences, creating a call and repeat quality to the speaking, calling, chanting and singing. This exercise will further enhance the relationship of the spoken voice and its creativity to the sung voice.

Building the voice further

Feel it first

If you have a piano nearby then use the notes as a guide. If not, there are musical scale apps which work just as well. The scale is to align ourselves with the notes we may wish to play with. Although we are fixing the note in the first instance, there will be exploration around the notes later in the exercise.

- Hum the musical note middle C.
- Now hum the musical note D.
- Now hum the musical note E.
- Now hum the musical note F.
- Now hum the musical note G.
- Now hum the musical note A.
- And finally hum the musical note B.
- Now let us revisit the musical notes set out above on the vowel sound AH as in car, keeping the volume levels low. If 10 is the loudest then perhaps imagine the humming sound stays around level 3 or 4.
- The aim is to *feel* your voice rather than push or present the sound. Try to avoid singing the sound; the suggestion would be more of intoning on the one note, without vibrato.
- Now sound the AH vowel to the musical note middle C, and imagine the colour red and that it sits at the base of the spine tailbone.
- Now sound the AH vowel to the musical note D, and imagine the colour orange, and that it sits in the sacral area just below the belly button.
- Now sound the AH vowel to the musical note E, and imagine the colour yellow, and that this sits in the solar plexus between the stomach area and the lungs.
- Now sound the AH vowel to the musical note F, and imagine the colour green, and this sits in the heart area and radiates between the upper lung and heart cavities.
- Now sound the AH vowel to the musical note G, and imagine the colour blue, and that it sits in the throat area around the larynx.
- Now sound the AH vowel to the musical note A, and imagine the colour indigo and this sits in the brow of the forehead.

- Finally, sound the AH vowel to the musical note B, and imagine the colour gold or white and this sits in the crown of the head.

- Continue this exercise playing with a variety of vowel sounds that explore the imaginary colour coming from the corresponding part of your body.

- Now allow yourself the possibility of other colours and vowel sounds that move away from this structure. Perhaps try painting a picture on the ceiling of your room with all the colours you have explored and perhaps many more that come to your mind. Perhaps the sound comes from other parts of your body.

Understand it

The sounds and exercises set out above use something known as the 'chakras', a Sanskrit word meaning 'wheel'. Chakras are seen as spinning wheels of light within the body. The exercise and image is useful and is not based upon any religious beliefs but energies within the body. It can be a useful way to explore placement of sound, resonance, intoning and tune, building the voice further, coupled with the use of the imagery to allow the creative part of the brain space to explore. The most well-known chakra is the solar plexus. This is a complex network of nerves (a nerve plexus) in the abdomen, sitting behind the stomach and in front of the diaphragm, level with the first lumbar vertebra.

Practise it

Practise the above sequence as a warm-up. Try this in three different ways:

- Lying down
- Sitting on a chair
- Standing up

In each of these also explore the spheres of the three rings of light and sound: *The self, At arm's length* and *To the world.*

Tips for teachers

The intoning chakras exercise above can take some time to develop; however, it is a good way to explore intoning the sound as well as placing the sound. In each note and corresponding colour you could spend as long as 2–4 minutes per note and colour. Explore with further vowels such as: ee, aye, eye, oh, oo, or even the corresponding vowel sounds that would align with the chakras, such as: uh, oo, oh, eye, aye, ee. The student may see the chakras or wheels on the body in different colours. It may be that you ask them to decide on their own colours. The spheres of light help 'see' the colours spiral out of the body into space.

Intone the text

Feel it first

Here are some exercises to activate areas in order to place the sound. To intone a sound, say a vowel on one note and extend the length of the note. Allow the shape of your mouth to change but always keep on the same note in this exercise.

- Stand in neutral and then move to N+.

- Intone the OO sound and say it on one note. Your lips will be rounded for this sound.

- Now intone that note and move the lips from the lip-rounded position to a smile or lip spreading.

- Stay on the same note and vowel for a while.

What happens to its sound?

Can you feel and hear how it changes the vowel sound?

How does it feel?

- Intone the sound EE and then intone the sound on one note, any note, you choose.

- Speak the OO vowel sound, then intone it and try placing the sound in the nasal area.

- Now speak the AH vowel sound, then intone it, and then change the shape of your mouth and notice where the sound rests.

- Next speak the AW sound and intone it, then send the sound to the head.

Does the sound feel and sound stronger in your chest, or the back or your nasal area?

This allows you to learn where to place sound.

Understand it

What is meant by intoning the text? What actually is intoning? Is it singing? Or is it speaking on one note? Is there any vibrato? The definition of intoning means to speak or recite with as little pitch variance as possible. Or perhaps a better way to think of it is to make speech sound like song, and song sound like speech, or to speak in monotones. This is often known as plainsong in psalms, canticles and Gregorian chants; it is used in liturgies which form a natural rhythm of speech, and is practised in Greek chorus speeches which are most effective in an ensemble.

It allows the actor to feel the colour of their voice come alive, using vowels to elongate the length of sound, creating the space and energy that sits between speech and song. The use of intoning text, especially verse, moving from speech to song has long been performed during the plays in Greek history. The Greek poetry and plays of Sophocles, Aeschylus and Euripides, and later those of the Roman poet Ovid, urge the text to often become intoned, calling for a greater depth of sound, moving from speech to song and somewhere in between, creating a heightened sense of the text. Nowadays the use of choral speaking to have an efficacy of truth means intoning can feel false, or less truthful. Finding the balance between speech and song, used to minimal effect, can have a greater impact on the audience and is a good vocal training skill.

Practise it

Intone on one or two notes with the sentences below.

> Hello my name is ...
> I live in ...
> I like to ...
> For Christmas I want ...
> My friend's/dog's/cat's/rabbit's/hamster's name is ...
> I want to be ...
> For my birthday I want ...

Speak Sonnet 8 by William Shakespeare below and intone the words using only two, perhaps three, notes of speech, running them into a song-like quality, without vibrato.

> Music to hear, why hear'st thou music sadly?
> Sweets with sweets war not, joy delights in joy;
> Why lov'st thou that which thou receiv'st not gladly,
> Or else receiv'st with pleasure thine annoy?
> If the true concord of well-tuned sounds
> By unions married, do offend thine ear,
> They do but sweetly chide thee, who confounds
> In singleness the parts that thou shouldst bear:
> Mark how one string, sweet husband to another,
> Strikes each in each by mutual ordering,
> Resembling sire, and child, and happy mother,
> Who all in one, one pleasing note do sing:

Whose speechless song being many, seeming one,
Sings this to thee: 'Thou single wilt prove none'.

Tips for teachers

The opening chorus speech from *The Oresteia* by
Aeschylus is a useful text to explore the intoning quality of
voice further. It is a long chorus speech; here are the first
four lines:

> Ten years ago, the sons of Atreus,
> Menelaus and Agamemnon,
> Both divine kings,
> Sailed across the sea to punish Priam.

Vowels and their modification, in and out of fashion

What is vowel modification? And how and when should it be used?
Why does my singing teacher insist upon this for singing and not for
speech, and should a vowel be so modified from speech to song?
Does the character lose authenticity if they change the vowel to
accommodate the singing?

Vowel modification is a somewhat outdated way of singing,
and can change the shape and meaning of the words, but
it is a recognized way of singing for some choirs in order to
accommodate the spoken pronunciation of a word to a shape
that is more easily sung. There is an adjustment to the way a
vowel is shaped that shifts to produce a more pleasing sound in
song. Classically trained singers use what's called the pure or tall
vowel, as the singing voice is generally thought to be more
interesting and beautiful to listen to than the actual words that

are sung. And, of course, with some operas, the beauty of the sung voice can be so emotionally charged that it can move you; even though you cannot understand what is being sung, it may be enough to lift you to an emotional state. However, in musical theatre the words and storytelling are far more important in order to drive the narrative forward and in a way that is accessible for everyone to understand.

Feel it first

- Stand in neutral, then move to N+.
- Sing a verse from an American song.
- Now speak that song in your own accent. *What do you notice about the vowels?*
- Now sing an English song. *Are you trying to give it an American accent?*
- Next speak the American song and blend the accent into singing it with an American accent.
- Then speak the English song and blend the accent into singing it with an English accent. You will find this harder than you think.

Understand it

An example of vowel modification would be the word 'company' in the musical *Company* by Stephen Sondheim. The vowel at the end of the word, *ee*, is often modified, so that some vocal coaches have been known to suggest it is sung as an ay, or 'companay'. However, striking a balance is more suitable, especially when the actor moves back to speech.

There is, of course, an understanding that some element of vowel change or modification needs to takes place in order for the laryngeal setting to be healthy for the singer; however, the modification can be taken too far. If we imagine that singing is like heightened speech, then there is always a slight modification from everyday speech to heightened speech; therefore, can we not admit that a slight adjustment for song may be possible too? A more appropriate way to help the MTP is to use the vowel modification as an exercise to get the correct position for the larynx, then change the shape of the mouth, and where possible bring the same quality into speech, so that there is a blending quality between the singer and the speaker. The word *love*, for example, can be explored as the word *lahv* to open up the sound creating more resonance. On the other hand, we have to be careful that this doesn't affect accent. There is nothing worse than listening to an actor speak a line with an English accent, as in *My Fair Lady* by Alan Jay Lerner, and then sing with modified vowels so much that they sound American; equally, to speak with a New York accent for the musical *Guys and Dolls* by Frank Loesser, and then sing in General American! Blending the vowels between speech and song is as far as modification needs to go, and this helps the application of the integrated performer.

American musicals are written for an American laryngeal setting, which naturally sits slightly higher than the British larynx in speech and song. Therefore, in songs such as 'I Believe' from the musical *Book of Mormon*, the /ee/ sound is at its highest, and can be difficult for many British male actors to accomplish well. The natural tendency would be to sing the EE sound as an AYE vowel sound. The aim is to blend the speaking vowels slightly to the singing vowels without compromising the sense or the accent. If the definitive rule is to sing the EE sound so strongly, then I would suggest British actors should spend as much time as possible speaking in the American accent to allow time to shift to one that feels and sounds more natural. Of course, the adjustment is very dependent on the accent of the musical, the director's style and choice and also what the musical director would be happy with. It can be harder for some singers to stay in tune, especially during the passaggio if they sing in the vowel as written, and therefore inexperience or lack of knowledge in the MTP often means they want to modify the vowel to get through the most difficult part of their range. Of course the idea of 'blending or mixing the voice' should allow for slight modification without constriction in the voice.

Practise it

- Speak the following sentence in your own accent: 'Today I saw a lovely rose by the sea, and it was purple and red.'
- Now sing the same sentence in any tune.

What do you feel? Are you modifying or changing the vowels to make it more pleasing to sing?

Or does it feel more comfortable to sing it slightly differently?

- Try speaking the same sentence above with an American accent.
- Then do the same with a British accent.
- Now sing it in another accent. *What do you notice?*

The glottal onset and its uses

There are many natural accents that use the glottal attack (Cockney, for example). This is where the vocal folds come together abruptly on words that begin with a vowel, where air pressure is built up underneath the vocal folds, and a popping sound occurs. This is often habitual and can be tiring on the voice: however, there are times when the glottal has its uses in both speech and song; firstly for accents and secondly at the beginning of a sung phrase where the music may dictate. In musicals like *Our House* a glottal onset allows a glide onto the vowel which is less tiring, and can help with the quality of the glottal onset.

Feel it first

- Start with a simple 'oh oh' or 'ah ah' as if you are gently telling off a small child. As the vocal folds come together you can feel a light pop-like quality. This can be tiring and something which you would wish to avoid.

- Now say 'yes'. You will notice how effortless this feels as the 'y' sound glides onto the rest of the word. This is known as a smooth onset.

- Look at the words below and use some gentle glottals as you say them aloud:
  - About
  - Around
  - Again
  - Overboard
  - Ostrich.

How does it feel? Do you notice if your voice feels tired?

- Now speak the same words again and this time use some breath before the word such as the /h/ sound. This will sound aspirate in front of each word. You will feel and sound breathy.

- Now this time speak the words again *thinking* the /h/ sound. This should produce what's known as simultaneous onset. This is a good way to explore the glottal and its habitual use.

- Now look at the following sentences; they all carry a word that begins with a vowel. Speak as many of the words with a glottal as possible.
  - About an apple an ostrich ate.
  - Even after everything.
  - I always allow an apple.
  - Oh, I allow animals every activity.

How does it feel? Tiring?

- Speak the same lines this time with the /h/ in front; this will feel very breathy.

- Now speak the same lines again, only this time *thinking* of the /h/ glide in front of the words.

How does it feel?

- This time try intoning or singing the earlier lines and glottalize only the first word of every line.

Understand it

The glottal when used safely and correctly can help the quality of sound – generally at the beginning of a vowel at the start of a singing phrase (not in all cases, but the music will tell you what is required) – and in many cultures the reliance on a small aspect of glottal executed safely can help with clarity of diction and ease of transition from spoken to sung voice. Judaic Aramaic singing is an example of marrying the sound of the glottal and mini yodelling.

Practise it

- Call out to someone across the room in space, use the glottal onset on the first sound or word.

- The second time slap your chest as an affirmation as you call out to them and glide onto the vowel.

- Gesture to them as you call out for a third time, experiment with pitch.

- On the fourth time tilt the larynx like a yodel as you gesture and call out to them, using pitch and gliding onto the vowel.

- For the fifth and final time call out and gesture adding the semi-tilt quality and sing the greeting out to them.

Suggested texts

Here are some suitable texts for you to try:

W. H. Auden, 'As I Walked Out One Evening'
Charles Bukowski, 'Bluebird'
Noel Coward, 'I've Been to a Marvellous Party'
Emily Dickinson, 'My Life Had Stood – a Loaded Gun'
Gerard Manley Hopkins, 'No Worst, There is None'
Ted Hughes, 'Ten Years Ago' (chorus speech from *The Oresteia*)
Henrik Ibsen, 'Doubt and Hope'
Rudyard Kipling, 'Recessional'
Marianne Moore, 'The Mind is an Enchanting Thing'
Sylvia Plath, 'Lady Lazarus'
Warsan Shire, 'For Women Who are Difficult to Love'
Victoria Wood, 'Giving Notes'

Further reading

Bunch, M. (1997), *Dynamics of the Singing Voice*, 4th edn, New York: Springer.

Chapman, J. L. (2006), *Singing: A Holistic Approach to Classical Voice*, Oxford: Plural Publishing.

Cook, O. (2008), *Singing with Your Own Voice*, London: Nick Hern Books.

Fisher, J. and G. Kayes (2016), *This is a Voice*, London: Welcome Collection.

Kayes, G. (2004), *Singing and the Actor*, 2nd edn, London: A & C Black.

Melton, J. with K. Tom (2012), *One Voice*, 2nd edn, Illinois: Waveland Press.

Rodgers, J. and F. Armstrong (2009), *Acting and Singing with Archetypes*, Montclair, NJ: Limelight Editions.

Spivey, N. and M. Saunders-Barton (2018), *Cross-Training in the Voice Studio*, San Diego, CA: Plural Publishing.

Stark, J. (2008), *Bel Canto: A History of Vocal Pedagogy*, University of Toronto Press.

4 Pitch and Tune

Keywords: pitch, encourage, range, tune

> To speak without colour is to speak without joy, and no one will listen. *GEORGIA O'KEEFE (REIMAGINED QUOTE)*

Introduction

What is pitch and tune within a speaking voice? Just imagine a person with very little pitch and tune in their speaking voice; perhaps you know someone whose voice lacks pitch variety so that listening to them makes you want to sleep. You may have heard your voice teachers saying 'monotony is mundane'. Well in all aspects of our speaking voice, from the performative voice to the social voice, as professional voice users, we should encourage the use of more colour, pitch and tune for vocal variety. The MTP needs to use *more* pitch variety in their speaking voice as the energy from speech to song requires brightness which is very rarely naturalistic, and more often than not is considered heightened speech.

In this chapter, we aim to move from building the voice and its emotional connection, to the exploration of pitch variety in everyday speech, performance speech and heightened speech, and to further develop that pitch into speech for stage in musicals. You will notice that in many plays today, speech is often more naturalistic, although if we think of the Greek plays, of Shakespeare, of pantomime and of music hall, the speech is heightened much like that of a musical! The pitch is often extreme to signpost the storyline in a way that is not done in plays, which are more naturalistic.

The use of pitch and its extremes from low notes to high notes is important to both speech and song. By exploring the musical notes within our speaking voice, we are often able to extend a greater degree of pitch within our singing voice too. The actor and voice specialist Roy Hart utilized his voice to vocal extremes in pitch for speech-singing or *sprechen spiel*, which allowed a greater degree of pitch through the experimentation and playfulness of voice. The Italians also are known for their incredible pitch variance, as are the Welsh.

Extreme pitch variation is used for characters such as Miss Hannagan from *Annie*, especially when the character is drunk, Willy Wonka from *Charlie and the Chocolate Factory*, some of the male characters in *Kinky Boots* and Gwynplaine from *The Grinning Man*. They all utilize the speaking voice to a much greater degree than would normally be expected in everyday speech.

Historically, the golden age musicals were written by skilled classical writers of music. Cole Porter, for example, was also a singer himself, singing in his own a cappella group. Many writers had also previously worked under the German classification known as the FACH system, the classification used at that time to indicate the weight, colour and range of voices. This understanding helped shape how to write for singers and their range.

The scores were written for stars of the day in musicals such as Cole Porter's *Anything Goes* (1934), *Kiss Me Kate* (1948 film), *High Society* (1956 film), and Ira and George Gershwin's *Shall We Dance?* (1937). This meant that the roles were often created for the movie stars of that time, who were not always naturally gifted singers: some were actors, some were pop stars, like Frank Sinatra, and others were predominantly dancers, like Fred Astaire.

Their vocal range in speech and song was much smaller than today's MTPs. In fact, in many of these movies, the actors often smoked, which may not have helped their singing range either. The vocal registers, and therefore the scores, were written to accommodate those stars. This of course plays a role in the pitch range and versatility of musicals through the ages. Kander and Ebb's *Chicago* (1975) and *Cabaret* (1966, with the film version in 1972) stayed within the speaking range of the singer and *perhaps* even lowered the pitch range for artists like Chita Rivera in the musical *Kiss of a Spider Woman* (1992). Musicals such as *Evita* (1978) by Andrew Lloyd Webber and Tim Rice, starring Elaine Paige and David Essex, and the musical *Cats* (1982) (again using Elaine Paige) used well-known pop stars to explore their musical range, further developing musicals that relied on those that could sing an extended range.

Musicals later began to be further informed by the mood of the world with Stephen Schwartz's *Godspell* (1970) and *Pippin* (1972). If you look at the vocal dexterity of the modern musicals, they are greatly influenced by the singing flicks and tricks of the pop singers of modern music. You can see the palpable influence of pop music in Stephen Schwartz's *Wicked* (2003), Dan Gillespie Sells and Tom Macraes' *Jamie the Musical* (2011), which has a strong pop sound and also a great strong Sheffield accent, *Bat out of Hell*, a rock musical by Jim Steinman, and of course Lin Manuel Miranda's *In the Heights* (2008) and *Hamilton* (2015), which uses accents and the dexterity of rap to enhance the speech qualities of the actors, which I will discuss further in Chapter 5. In all these musicals, the MTP must switch genres in their speaking range, from accents to rap.

This means the MTP must sing notes often out of their natural range, using the vocal dexterity of a pop performer (who may only use their voices to perform once a week, whereas the MTP is often performing eight shows per week, with a contract lasting up to a year at a time). Blending the speaking voice in pitch to the singing voice is, therefore, a necessary part of creating that pitch and tune understanding.

To develop the speaking range, it is useful to know where your voice naturally sits. *Does your voice have a deeper quality to it than say your friends of a similar age and gender?* If that is your natural setting then rejoice in that, rather than imposing any negative connotations that may have come from peers who, in the past, may have said your voice is too high or too low. Once you have established where your voice naturally sits, there are ways to further develop the pitch variance and tune to understand the mechanics behind it. Let's explore.

High and low: Playing with pitch

Feel it first

Pitch and tune (Video)

- Begin by standing in neutral, feet hip distance apart, knees soft, long torso, long neck, arms hanging gently by the side. Then check in with your sound by sirening up and down the scale. You make this sound with your tongue and soft palate, and explore your range up and down the scale.

- Keep the volume levels low, about 3–4.

- Still keeping the volume levels low, hum up and down the scale

- Now open to the EE vowel, sounding up and down the scale.

- Now sound the AYE vowel, sounding up and down the scale.

- Now sound the AH vowel, sounding up and down the scale.

- Now sound the vowel sequence OO EE OO EE OO.

- Now repeat the sequence going up a third each time.

- Now say yeah, yeah, yeah, playing each time with your pitch.

- Now say yah, yah, yah, playing each time with your pitch.

- Now say the OOH sound, and make it as interesting a sound as you can each time you say it.

- Point to something and say the OOH sound as if you've seen something wonderful. Now something terrible.

- Now make the vowel sound very short. OOH.

- Now make the vowel sound very long. OOOOOHHHH.

Count aloud the numbers from 1 to 10 using your full range for the low notes, right up to the high notes for the higher numbers. These high and low notes allow you to hear and feel what is going on in your larynx and what you perceive in sound. Now try these variations.

- Say the numbers 1 to 10, but varying the pitch. So 1 (up); 2 (down); 3 (up); 4 (down) and so on.

- Now say the days of the week with pitch variance for every other word. Monday (up); Tuesday (down) and so on.

- Now say the months of the year changing the pitch on every other month. January (up); February (down); March (up) and so on.

Understand it

The pitch of your voice is the result of the vocal folds' frequency when they vibrate. A higher note is produced when the vocal folds are lengthened and stretched thinly, and in the case of lower notes the vocal folds become slack and thicker as the tension is decreased by the crico-thyroids. Creating these high and low notes allows you to hear and feel what is going on in your larynx and what you perceive in sound.

Practise it

Here is a word list for smells.

Speak the words listed below, using a different vocal quality and pitch for each word. You will find the words are mostly onomatopoeic. In other words, the list resembles, suggests or sounds like the word being described, and allows you to instantly feel your pitch rise and fall with words; you may naturally do this anyway. This enhances the use of pitch quite effectively.

- Stinky
- Chocolate
- Smelly
- Cake
- Coffee
- Pooh
- Crumpets
- Cookies
- Stench.

Notice what is happening to your larynx.

Is it moving up? Or down? How does it feel?

Does it want to encourage you to explore pitch in other words?

High pitch words: try this word list to encourage further the higher pitch variance. These words are almost onomatopoeic, and they explore the upper register of your voice.

- Squeak
- High
- Heaven
- Sky
- Cheap

- Sweetie
- Twinkle
- Star
- Fairy
- Princess Megan Sparkles.

What happens to the sense of the word if you do the opposite pitch?

Does it change the meaning or your intention because the pitch is different from the expected intention?

Notice what is happening to your larynx. *Is it moving up or down? How does it feel?*

Low pitch words: here are a list of words that are almost onomatopoeic. They explore the lower register of your voice, and again give you a sense of the word as you explore them.

- Rumble
- Thunder
- Dark
- Deep
- Hell
- Low
- Hole
- Ground
- Groan
- Moan.

What happens to the sense of the word if you do the opposite pitch?

Does it change the meaning or your intention because the pitch is different from the expected intention?

Notice what is happening to your larynx. *Is it moving up? Or down? How does it feel?*

Weather words for pitch range: here are a list of words to describe feelings regarding the weather. Speak the words and try to make yourself or someone else grasp the feelings of the word you are trying to convey.

- Cold
- Warm
- Hot
- Chilly
- Frosty
- Rainy
- Freezing.

Notice what is happening to your larynx.

Is it moving up? Or down? How does it feel in your voice?

How does it feel in your body? Can you feel or hear a different pitch quality to your voice in each of these exercises?

You can always record yourself, then play the recording back. Sometimes what we feel is not always heard by our ear automatically. The recording may convince you of the greater variety you have explored and created.

Practise it further

The next exercises aim to establish pitch within sentences.

Here are some sentences for low pitch and sad feelings:

- I worked 300 hours last week.
- I am unhappy with my life.
- The poor man was taken to hospital with a broken leg.
- The rocket plummeted to earth.
- The black hole ate up the dog.
- The man died after three hours in surgery.

How does your voice feel? How do the sentences make you feel?

Do you feel you are communicating the sense of the line?

What happens if you change the pitch to a high set of notes, does it alter the sense?

Here are some sentences for high pitch, which are excitable and fun:

- The girl squealed with delight as she got the part in a musical.
- The man was happy to have won the lottery.
- The boy bounced up and down on the trampoline.
- The puppy was a lovely surprise.
- The woman waved her million pound cheque in the air.

How does your voice feel? Do the sentences make you feel happy? Excitable?

- Now speak these sentences and explore the opposite pitch; notice how the meaning and intention is changed.
- Perhaps speak a poem with as much pitch variance as you can, be creative and explore your range fully.
- Now speak the Chorus speech from Act 4 of *Henry V*.

Now entertain conjecture of a time
When creeping murmur and the poring dark
Fills the wide vessel of the universe.
From camp to camp, through the foul womb of night,
The hum of either army stilly sounds,
That the fixed sentinels almost receive
The secret whispers of each other's watch.
Fire answers fire, and through their paly flames
Each battle sees the other's umbered face.
Steed threatens steed, in high and boastful neighs

Piercing the night's dull ear; and from the tents
The armorers, accomplishing the knights,
With busy hammers closing rivets up,
Give dreadful note of preparation.
The country cocks do crow, the clocks do toll,
And, the third hour of drowsy morning name.
Proud of their numbers and secure in soul,
The confident and overlusty French
Do the low-rated English play at dice
And chide the cripple, tardy-gaited night,
Who like a foul and ugly witch doth limp
So tediously away.

Tips for teachers

A variation on a class I remember that David Carey
introduced me to: set the group a task to explore a piece of
text or poem extending the pitch range with a particular
purpose, perhaps using the song 'Ning, Nang, Nong' by
Spike Milligan, or 'Jabberwocky' by Lewis Carroll, for
example. Divide the group into two with one group telling
the story using the text as if to a group of five-year-olds. The
second group to imagine it like a news report. Both groups
show and tell. This further highlights the extremes of vocal
playfulness, pitch range and vocal variety, enhancing
intentions such as sarcasm and rudeness. Exploring pitch in
this way creates mood and intention, allowing the students
to explore, and they can then show each other the work.
With each of the words in the word lists you can add a
physical action. You could also develop a sound-scape in
exploration, to further develop the understanding of pitch
range. Using a gesture or movement to add to the exercise
further encourages the student to explore pitch and the
movement can be identified with the sound.

Building the pitch

To build the pitch we have to begin putting some of the sections explored in all previous chapters together. So far the exercises have been kept at a low-level volume settings of around 3 to 4. As we begin to build your sound, you will need to increase the volume levels perhaps to 6 to 7 as you use N+, using breath support, pitch and intoning.

Feel it first

- Begin standing in N+, keeping the C-shape from chest to chin with your hand, to maintain a sense that the larynx is in neutral. Then drop your arms.

- Take your fingers onto your ribs on an inhalation and then on exhalation release on the ff, ff, ff, ff sound. (Feel the internal intercostal muscles working. Isolation of muscles within the ribs means that there is less emphasis on abdominal breathing; it happens naturally, as we access the breath.)

- Now imagine you are about to yawn (the pre-yawn).

- Make the EE sound by intoning, using lip rounding for this, keeping the tongue-tip forward on the back of the lower teeth.

- Move from the EE sound to the OO sound with the tongue-tip on the lower teeth, moving back and forth from the OO sound to the EE sound. This allows the larynx to stay in neutral. (You may notice it sounds like the siren of an old-style ambulance or police car.)

- Now intone yeah, yeah, yeah. This is better than saying the word 'yes' as the /s/ stops the sound from continuing forward, therefore the open vowel sound carries forth.

- Now intone WAA, WAA, WAA, and feel a slight 'tilt' in the larynx, much like a mini yodel.

Understand it

Using some singing exercises helps explore the range, pitch and tune within the speaking voice. The singing voice is primitive, and we play with pitch and tune, hum and sing without even being aware of it. The first sounds a baby makes are not words but pitch and babble. It's instinctive, and sounds wonderful, exploring and playing with pitch and tune. We start to lose a sense that we can sing quite early on in our childhood, and that singing should be saved for the very best of singers. We begin to close down our pitch and use the verbal side of communication rather than the playful sing-song quality that is within us all.

Pitch is not gender specific, as singers like Ed Sheeran and Sam Smith, who use high notes and soft mellow tones, demonstrate. The possibilities of pitch and tune to be explored in the speaking voice demonstrates how expressive an actor can be.

A female example of excellent pitch range in speech would be Dame Maggie Smith and the characters she has played. The mastery of use of pitch range and the application to character fully explores the notion of playing with the pitch and tune of text, which can colour the words, providing the listener with a greater degree of clarity. This can add gravitas to characters you are playing, and the actor's fuller vocal range allows them to continue to work well into later age. A male example of excellent pitch range, and articulation so exquisitely executed, is the late comic actor Kenneth Williams.

Practise it

- Begin standing in neutral then move to N+. Engage with the imagery of angel wings on your back as you raise your arms above your head and slowly bring them to elbow height. Imagine you have some resistance to your arms.

- Remember to engage with the image of angels swimming through syrup, and feel the big C from chin to chest.

- Imagine you are about to yawn.

- Now yawn and enjoy the feeling.

- Start with the sustained ee sound.

- Now make the sound ee, use some lip rounding for this sound.

- Now engage the ribs by an excited breath, on the inhalation. The breath should not be audible, but it should feel like an excited sound, exhale for fff, fff, fff, fff, fff.

- Now make the huvvv, huvvv sound (the vvv stops too much air escaping and helps to regulate the air pressure).

- Activate the middle voice, or the chest voice, with whoops of joy. The chin should feel lifted, the eyes slightly higher than eye line. The whoops of joy should feel like you are at a rock concert and you are enjoying whooping for your favourite band or singer.

  Can you feel your larynx tilt slightly? Or can you feel it move up and down?

- Try and make a sound like a sad dog: woo, woo, woo, woo, woo.

- Try and make a sound like a cat, meow, meow,, meow meow, meow, and allow the lips to be rounded.

- Explore this further by using your pitch range.

- Now imagine you are a dramatic opera singer, and produce an ooh sound, whilst dropping the jaw into a relaxed state.

- The ooh sound from high to low in register can be explored but keep the larynx in neutral.

- Adopt the lip rounding shape as in the ooh, as this effectively lowers the larynx. This also lengthens the vocal tract, and you will have more overtones in the sound quality in your speaking voice, which will have more overall added resonance and timbre.

- Now try the vowel sequences:

  - Oo wah oo

  - Oo wee oo wee

  - Oo way oo way

  - Oo woh oo who.

- When you next get the opportunity, sing in the shower, then speak in the shower.

  How does your voice feel? How does it sound?

Tips for teachers

If you find that some students have some tension in their tongue, then suggest they stretch the tongue forward as far as they can, keeping the tongue behind the bottom teeth as they do this and anchoring the neck by pushing against their forehead with their fingers; this will stabilize the sternocleidomastoids. The larynx should be in a relaxed neutral position, although sometimes it may rise or lower; this is fine so long as you are not forcing it up or down. If the student's larynx raises, just get them to swallow a few times afterwards to bring it back to neutral.

Chants and text in sense and nonsense

What is chanting? Chanting may be considered a heightened form of speech that was largely used in the Middle Ages in a religious context. (The Gregorian chant, for example, uses very few notes and the words are often produced as speak-singing, a form of singing which involves some of the characteristics of the speaking voice.) There are generally very few notes, or very simple melodies, which can range from choral song, to responsorial chanting, to unison, solo and ensemble. Various cultures still use a form of chanting to orally tell the myths and stories of their ancestors' past, each outlining lessons for the younger generation.

Feel it first

Repeat these over and over adding harmonies. This is quiet work, as a good cool down, or a gathering and centring.

Intoning chant inspired by Buddhist chants:

Om Mani pandei um
Om Mani pandei um

Om Mani Pandei Umm

Om ma - ni pan-dei umm, om ma - ni pan-dei umm.

Figure 4.1 Om Mani pandei um: a Buddhist chant.

Chant inspired by Hindi chants:

Tomtare twotare torre soh ha
Tomtare twotare torre soh ha

Tomtare Twotare

Tom - ta - re, two - ta - re, to - rre soh - ha.

Figure 4.2 Tomtare twotare torre soh ha: a Hindi chant.

Understand it

The traditional chants of the indigenous peoples of Native America, Aboriginal peoples in Australia, Africa, and South and Central America, and across Europe are examples of cultural identities that share the love of speak-singing to tell stories. The Swedish 'Kulning', which uses a sound for calling animals across acres of land, follows the similar Celtic sounds used in keening, or crying, when a loved one has died.

Chants have been used for thousands of years by many cultures across the world, and many still do chant. Some use them for ritualistic song and dance to explore both life on earth or moving on to another spiritual plane. Then there are the hardship chants of union workers, slave chants, and chants that speak to a higher being in a more standardized religious context. Whatever the original reason, the chants and songs set out here are there to explore sound and movement in this context.

The use of chanting to explore sound is well recognized as a form of warming up the voice. The simple note quality means the voice is not overstimulated until other forms of warm-up exercise have been realized. Chanting or intoning is often an easy way to explore the sound and the ensemble quality of a group, as it requires listening skills as well as the performative element.

Practise it

Try these various chants.

Intoning chant inspired by workers' rights and unions:

> Step by step I follow the march.
> One by one we walk the line.
> Step by step we overcome.
> One by one we rise.

Figure 4.3 Step By Step: a workers' chant.

Intoning chant inspired by the tribes of the Navahos:

Hey ho hey ya, wolf and eagle are one.
Hi ho hi ya, the spirits of the plain.
Tee da tee da, their journey is conjoined.
So ha see ha, my heart is full of pain.

Figure 4.4 Hey ho hey ya: Navaho tribal chant.

Intoning chant inspired by students from Macedonia:

Legnei ammarow mori otkor
Yakult amarrow lurei

Figure 4.5 Legnei ammarow: a Macedonian student chant.

Tips for teachers

If any of these are used as a warm-up, then it is useful to place the sound. If used as a group chant, then it is a good chance to see when the group decides it will end. (For this you will need to get them to close their eyes.) The use of football chants encourages the chanting sounds which both male and female students can enjoy with a call and response theme. Or encourage them to create their own chant which they must teach their group. The chants themselves can go on for as long as is required and I have often allowed groups to go on as long as 30 minutes. By the end of the session the voice is clear, warm and able to take on greater tasks. These can also be used as a cool down after a particular long session.

All the chants and proverbs are inspired by various cultures; they have been changed or built upon in order to enhance my own practice.

Further reading

Bunch, M. (1997), *Dynamics of the Singing Voice*, 4th edn, New York: Springer.

Carey, D. and R. Carey Clark (2008), *Vocal Arts Workbook and DVD*, London: Methuen Drama.

Estill, J. (1992), 'Basic figures and exercise manual'. From *A User's Guide to Voice Quality*, Pittsburgh, PA: Estill voice training systems.

Fisher, J. and G. Kayes (2016), *This is a Voice*, London: Welcome Collection.

Garfield Davies, D. and A. F. Jahn (1999), *Care of the Professional Voice*, Oxford: Butterworth Heinemann.

Lessac, A. (1967), *The Use and Training of the Human Voice: A Bio-dynamic Approach to Vocal Life*, 2nd edn, New York: McGraw-Hill.

Meir, P. (2011), *Accents and Dialects for Stage and Screen*, Lawrence, KA: Paul Meir Dialect Services.

Melton, J. with K. Tom (2012), *One Voice*, 2nd edn, Illinois: Waveland Press.

Robison, K. (2000), *The Actor Sings*, Portsmouth: Heinemann.

5 Articulation

Keywords: consonants, isolate, alliteration, articulation, activate, awaken

If you stop listening, the tongue will do the talking. *NATIVE AMERICAN PROVERB*

Introduction

What is meant by good dynamic articulation? What are the articulators and how can we use them to great effect? Voice and singing teachers may often say, 'I need to hear clearer diction', 'Continue to work on dynamic articulation', 'I can't hear the precision of consonants' and so on. It is important to understand how those sounds can be arrived at, how to isolate various muscles, and further to that, how to awaken the articulators without causing tension.

In this chapter, the aim is to bring many elements of the voice together, in order to develop your knowledge of creative articulation, and to enhance the words to such a height that you can learn to explore text in an imaginative and exciting way: that squeezes out the juice of most words, letting them land on the listener's ear.

Articulators

There are several articulators, some of which are movable, such as the vocal folds (also known as the vocal chords), the lips, the tongue, the velum (soft palate), the uvula, the pharynx and the jaw (mandible). The tongue is the most movable and mobile of the articulators. Then there are the fixed articulators which are the hard palate, the teeth and the alveolar ridge. Awakening and isolating these articulators with the power source of the breath is key to unlocking dynamic articulation and precise diction. To quote the March Hare from Lewis Carroll's *Alice in Wonderland*, 'you should say what you mean'.

Feel it first

Now say puh as in the /p/ sound.

- Now say buh as in the /b/ sound. Perhaps you can feel the vibrations in your throat area. Notice that the puh sound has air that is expired and yet the sound is voiceless, that is, it has no sound but the expiration of breath.
- Now say tuh as in the /t/ sound.
- Now say duh as in the /d/ sound.
- Now say kuh as in the /k/ sound.
- Now say guh as in the /g/ sound.

Understand it

With regards to articulation, consonants are thought to be more important for the delivery of text in speech, whereas vowels are considered more important in singing, because of the sustained sound of the vowel. This historical belief is a hangover from the Bel Canto model of classical singing, where the 'voice beautiful' was considered more important than the words. I would of course argue that unless we can hear the words of both speech and song then it becomes nonsense and merely a series of flicks and tricks to wash over the listener. Musical theatre relies principally on the story being told through speech, song and dance. The story is the essence; never more so than in the musicals of Stephen Sondheim.

Practise it

- Place one hand on your throat area repeating the exercise above by voicing the /b/ sound. You will begin to recognize that one sound vibrates in the larynx as you awaken and isolate the /b/ sound. You may be able to feel the resonance or vibrations and hear the sound.

- For the consonants t, k, f, p and s, the vocal folds are open and so they are voiceless sounds.

- For the consonants d, g, v, b and z, the vocal folds are closed and so they are voiced sounds.

- Try the paired combinations now: pb, td, kg, sz and fv. You will notice that they come in pairs, one is voiced and one is voiceless; however, the two sounds are made in the same place.

- Try the voiceless combination of puh, tuh and kuh. I am sure you will have noticed that this combination starts at the front of the mouth with the bilabial plosive (see section on consonants and various plosives later in this chapter), puh then moves to the alveolar plosive tuh in the middle of the mouth and finally the velar plosive kuh at the back of the mouth.

- Say and notice the front of the mouth puh.

- Say and notice the middle of the mouth tuh.

- Say and notice the back of the mouth kuh.

Now feel the *voiced* sounds of front, middle and back of the mouth.

- Say and notice buh at the front of the mouth.

- Say and notice duh at the middle of the mouth.

- Say and notice guh at the back of the mouth.

- Now try this combination, puh tuh kuh, puh tuh kuh, getting faster and faster all the while keeping the clarity of each consonant.

- Now try the combination, buh duh guh, buh duh guh, over and over getting faster and faster, trying to keep the integrity of the consonant.

Feel it first

The lip gym (Video)

Where would we be without the lips? The tongue and jaw would surely have to work hard in order to make sound, so let us activate and awaken the lips.

- Isolate the top lip and raise it much like a theatrical curtain saying 'tah dah' as you raise it.
- Now try raising the top lip on one side like Elvis Presley and say 'ah ha'.
- Now try the other side and say 'er' as if you don't like someone, much like a sneer.
- Now imagine you have just tasted a lemon, and say 'eeyeugh!', becoming lemon-faced, sour-faced or lemon-lipped. Practise this with a partner or in the mirror while mouthing the words or sounds you are making.
- Now pucker up and make the sounds of lips kissing, as if trying to get the attention of a dog or cat.

Lip trills are where the lips have some tension in them and air is forced through, creating a horse-like lip trill sound.

- Now isolate lip trills without sound.
- Now try the horse lip trills with sound – you can place one hand on your throat or your larynx area to feel the sound you create.
- Try the 3-minute lip trill exercise – try the horse trills for 3 minutes.
- Now lip trill a song; a suggestion could be 'Happy birthday'.

Understand it

You may feel that your lips are fuller, larger or itchy. This feeling will be blood flowing to the lip area as you awaken the muscles, reaching the lips causing them to tickle or feel a little itchy. This shows them working out at the lip gym.

Practise it

- Repeat the above exercises every day whilst doing things around the house, such as putting on the kettle, or getting yourself ready. Ten minutes per day will help with your articulation.

Feel it first

The jaw spa (Video)

Often tension can creep into the jaw when you are working on articulation, or you may have experienced jaw tension at other times, so it is important to allow time in your warm-up for releasing any jaw and lip tension. Imagine you are at a jaw spa. The exercises that follow are to isolate the lips so that they are loose and released; this will help relax and isolate the jaw from the lips too. Try to disengage the lips, allowing for sloppy diction.

- Brush down the sides of your jaw with your hands, and then say the following sentences with relaxed sloppy articulation:

  - Say 'Oh no', then brush down the jaw with your hands.

  - Next say 'No I can't', then brush down the jaw.

  - Continue with, 'Sorry', then brush down the jaw.

  - Be rude and say, 'Nah I don't think so', then brush down the jaw.

  - Now be really rude: 'No I don't want to'.

How does your jaw feel? Is it more relaxed?

Are you at least aware of your jaw?

Understand it

Jaw tension happens when we clamp down too hard without being aware of it. Sometimes we can do it in our sleep, sometimes when we are upset or stressed, angry or frustrated. This often leads to tension in the neck, larynx and shoulders, tongue and jaw. Serious jaw tension leads to Temporomandibular Joint Disorder (TMJ); this joint is where the lower jaw (mandible) and the skull connect. Releasing jaw tension through the exercises above creates an awareness to consider it when warming up; this awareness can have a positive impact on the tongue and jaw, allowing a greater sense of freedom for the tongue to do its job. The blood flow at the base of the skull (the atlanto-occipital joint) can be shortened through poor posture and tension and, when compromised, can produce headaches and jaw tension.

Practise it

- In pairs, one of you lie down on the floor on your front, with your forehead on your hands, and place a tissue under your mouth, then allow the jaw and tongue to completely relax. Your partner will gently massage the shoulders and then tap all over the back. This is a 3-minute exercise and you will undoubtedly dribble (that is what the tissue is for); how do your jaw and lips feel? Does your facial mask feel relaxed?

- Stand up, keeping your face relaxed even if you dribble; this will allow you to feel the release of tension in your jaw and potentially your shoulders.

- Raise and lower the shoulders, then try and lower them further towards your feet.

- Now press the thumbs of both hands under your chin and feel your tongue as you swallow. Move the tongue around in the mouth keeping your thumbs under your chin and begin to massage this area.

- Try pulling some of your skin away around the neck and larynx area. This will make you aware of any tension.

- Place your thumb under your jaw and give it some pressure or resistance, whilst trying to open the jaw, almost as if the jaw can only open and close using the thumb.

- Feel your fingers and thumbs move along the lower jaw line and into the back of the neck and then follow the line into the space between head and neck. This space or groove is known as the atlanto-occipital joint at the top of the cervical vertebrae (where the top of the spine meets the skull).

- Massage this area with your fingers.

- Imagine a picture of an eye on the back of your neck that can see the world.

- Nod your head (yes) several times, then shake it (no) several times.

- Now use your fingers to massage into this space, increasing some blood flow.

- Circle your nose several times both clockwise and anti-clockwise, then make the shape of a cross. Again this increases body awareness and isolates different muscles and joints, in the neck and jaw.

- Hold the jaw with one hand and hold the back of the head with the other and say a line of text. Try to isolate the tongue so that you are aware of when the jaw wants to take over the work of the tongue. *Does the lower jaw want to move much?*

- With a relaxed and loose jaw, voice the /huh/ sound without using the lips or jaw; begin this with the tongue on the floor of the mouth.

- Now start with the /nuh/ sound and allow the tongue to reach up to the roof of the mouth and then gently control it by letting the tongue down to the floor of the mouth. You can practise this with a mirror.

- Finally smile, because when you smile you release tension in your jaw.

How does your jaw feel? Does it want to awaken, engage or get involved?

What about your tongue, does it feel like it is working harder?

Feel it first

Tongue-tastic (Video)

- Poke out your tongue with the lips closed around the tongue, and point the tongue up and down and side to side Imagine your tongue is an animal in a cave, looking outside for the first time. You may feel your neck wishing to engage, so occasionally either place your finger on your chin, in order to feel some resistance to it, or hold the back of the neck.

- Continue to point the tongue, up and down and side to side, as you awaken the tongue animal within.

- Point the tongue, with the mouth open and the lips relaxed. Imagine you have a fat tongue, then a thin tongue, and watch yourself in a mirror.

- Circle the tongue inside the right cheek clockwise, then try anti-clockwise; then move the tongue to the left side of the mouth and do the same exercise on the left side.

- Now try the same exercise with your tongue outside the mouth.

Understand it

There are eight muscles of the tongue, four are the intrinsic muscles and four are the extrinsic muscles. The intrinsic muscles aim to change the *shape* of the tongue, as in the fat tongue/thin tongue shape you made earlier. The extrinsic muscles aim to change the *position* of the tongue, as in pointing the tongue in and out of the mouth as you made earlier. The tongue is a fascinating muscle, divided into two parts throughout its length by what is known as the median septum; this is a partition running all the way along from the hyoid bone at the base of the tongue through to the tip. The tongue is also attached to the epiglottis, the skull and the frenulum. The frenulum is a membrane attached to the floor of the mouth and the underneath of the tongue. Sometimes this is short, causing some people literally to be tongue tied; however, with the right help it is possible that good exercises in muscularity can still allow for greater control and dynamic articulation. Learning to awaken and isolate the tongue can cause neck tension, so be mindful that you continue to have a long neck with the chin slightly tucked under and to imagine the open eye on the back your neck.

Practise it

- Blow a raspberry with your tongue out– try this with sound and without sound.

- Blow the raspberry to a tune, or create your own language only using the raspberry blowing.

- Try the following exercises with and without a mirror. Always feel it first then notice in the mirror what you are doing with your tongue and neck, jaw and shoulders.

    ○ Now try curling the tongue into different shapes.

    ○ Take the tip of the tongue and let it touch the bottom teeth, roll the body of the tongue forward and out, then bring the body of the tongue down and back. I like to call this the tongue wave. The tongue wave helps release tension, so take the tip of your tongue behind the bottom teeth and push the body of the tongue out; the tongue looks like an ocean wave when looking at it sideways.

- ○ Activate the tongue wave bringing it in and out of the mouth and give it a sound. Be mindful that your jaw and neck do not become engaged. Look at yourself in the mirror as you do this. It may sound a little like a baby making sound; that's a good sign.
- ○ Try different sounds whilst making the tongue wave.

How does your tongue feel? Is your tongue aching?

Does your neck ache, has it been trying to get in on the action?

Does your neck want to come forward? Do you have a pigeon neck when doing this exercise? Be mindful if the neck or jaw wants to get involved. Remind them it is not their turn.

Tips for teachers

Here are a few 3-minute challenges to get the group working solo, in pairs and some group work. This is a series of quick and fun exercises which draw attention to specific areas associated with articulation. Some young students will find this a challenge and yet it will improve their articulation without drawing too much attention to lazy tongue, lips or tight jaws.

- 3-minute self-massage on the face, lips, jaw and head.
- 3-minute neck release with the nose working in semi-circles from ear to ear, then nose crosses, nose writing names in the air, nose full circles.
- 3 minutes with lips holding a pen or carrot or an object of similar quality: feel the muscles within the lips as they hold the object, then release a bit without dropping it.

- 3 minutes speaking ventriloquist: in pairs one student stands behind the other and speaks and the person in front becomes the mouthpiece.
- 3 minutes singing ventriloquist, as above.
- 3-minute chat in pairs: one is the mouthpiece whilst the other partner makes sounds and noises and speech, and then swap over. In class you're observing only the mouthpiece in order to see an improvement of a working mouth and tongue. The person that is speaking needs to work hard in order for the class to hear what is being said, as the 'dummy' must mouth very well the words being said. This teaches the students listening and observation skills.

Bone prop and how to use it

Fruit and vegetable exercises (pre-bone prop)

I like to begin the training of articulation with a carrot in the mouth or a slice of cucumber. This allows you to see how hard you may grip the aforementioned vegetable by showing the tooth marks as you bite down. If the vegetable has very strong teeth marks, perhaps you are biting down too hard! You will need five pieces of carrot (or other fruit or vegetables) about the size of a finger.

Feel it first

Place a small piece of carrot in the mouth so that some of it sticks out; now begin with the sounds below:

- Ba, ba, ba, bay, bee, boo
- Da, da, da, day, dee, doo
- Fa, fa, fa, fay, fee, foo

- Ga, ga, ga, gay, gee, goo
- Ja, ja, ja, jay, jee, joo
- Ka, ka, ka, kay, kee, koo
- La, la, la, lay, lee, loo
- Ma, ma, ma, may, mee, moo
- Na, na, na, nay, nee, noo
- Pa, pa, pa, pay, pee, poo
- Ra, ra, ra, ray, ree, roo
- Sa, sa, sa, say, see, soo
- Sha, sha, sha, shay, she, shoo
- Ta, ta, ta, tay, tee, too
- Va, va, va, vay, vee, voo
- Za, za, za, zay, zee, zoo.

Are there tooth marks on the carrot?

Have you over-activated the jaw?

- Repeat the exercises again with a new piece of vegetable and notice if the tooth marks become less indented.
- See if you can release the grip on the carrot and still make a good strong sound.
- Now lay all the carrots out in a row and see from carrot 1 to carrot 5 if the marks are less prominent. This is a lovely visual way of seeing evidence of jaw gripping and its release as the exercise moves forward. You may find your jaw aches as it releases its hold. This will be evidence on how much work it does for you which is not always so useful, as it has been gripping the words so hard.

Are you gripping less now?

Now we can introduce the bone prop, revisiting the same exercises as above. You are now familiar with the concept of speaking with an object in your mouth. You may notice a change with and without the bone prop. The likelihood is that you will feel an incredible difference in the mouth, the sound will feel more forward and the space created will feel open, relaxed and effortless. Your speech and song has new tone and resonance.

Understand it

The use of the bone prop has at times in the teaching of voice been a contentious one. It has been in and out of fashion when training actors, as there was a time when a large cork was used in the mouth to create space, but that seems too large, too harsh and could result in jaw tension. Many singing teachers use a finger or two to keep the opening of the mouth wide enough for the tongue to work. However, I have found that the use of the bone prop in training musical theatre students saves time and creates the right level of muscularity needed for singing and speaking, especially when using the bone prop after the vegetable work. I prefer to use the Morrison Bone Prop (see Appendix 2) as this is the most effective speech tool. It has a small groove for the teeth and allows the tongue to move the bone prop around in the mouth, without causing tension.

Consonants

Bilabial plosives

Feel it first

/p/ and /b/ are known as bilabial plosives. This means the two lips are brought together, forming an obstruction to the outgoing breath. Once some pressure has built up behind the lips, the obstruction is suddenly released by the lips opening like doors, and sound is produced. Depending on whether the vocal folds are vibrating or not, the sound will be either voiced or voiceless.

- Now say ppp pa/ ppp pa/ ppp pa/ ppp pa/ ppp pa/ voiceless.
- Now say bbb ba/ bbb ba/ bbb ba/ bbb ba/ bbb ba/ voiced.
- Now place your hand on your throat area and alternate between the two sounds of p and b. You can feel and hear the difference between the voiced and voiceless sounds. You can also try these exercises with a bone prop.

Understand it

Good articulation is less about changing your individual accent and more about communication. Actors, and in fact many other public figures, are expected to speak clearly and be understood, generally within a performative setting. Many politicians as well as celebrities, including footballers, branch out in their later careers into presenting for TV, and need to rely on good articulation in order to reach a wider audience than perhaps what is necessary for a social setting.

Try these unvoiced sounds in the *initial* (beginning), the *medial* (middle) or the *final* (end) position. You will notice that the bold lettering of the nonsense sentences is an indicator of the level of intensity needed for each word.

Practise it

- Words with **p** in the initial position: **P**ansies **p**artied and **p**ulsated **p**roactively in **p**airs.
- Words with **p** in the medial position: Hi**pp**y, ha**pp**y, chi**p**olatas, cam**p**ing, co**p**ing, car**p**ing.
- Words with **p** in the final position: Ho**p**e, ho**p**, car**p**, ta**p**, ti**p**, trollo**p**, lea**p**, grou**p**, shi**p**.

Now try these voiced sounds in the *initial*, *medial* or *final* position.

- Bbb ba/ bbb ba/ bbb ba/ bbb ba/ bbb ba/

- Initial: **B**lue **b**ulbs **b**loom **b**lossoming **b**eautifully.

- Medial: Ga**bb**y the go**b**lin wo**bb**les and ru**b**s the ta**bb**y.

- Final: Cheru**b** bo**b**s in a tu**b**.

Alveolar plosives

/t/ and /d/ are known as the alveolar plosives because on the out-breath the soft palate is raised and the blade of the tongue touches the alveolar ridge; the obstruction caused creates a build-up of pressure and release.

Practise it

Voiced /d/

- Initial: **D**ad **d**umped **d**irt in the **d**umpster.

- Medial: La**dd**ers and lu**dd**ites un**d**ulate un**d**er be**dd**ing.

- Final: Tire**d** bir**d** woun**d** the prou**d** woo**d**.

Voiceless /t/

- Initial: **T**iming a **t**une in **t**ime is **t**rying.

- Medial: Coun**t**ries ne**tt**ed ki**tt**y li**tt**er.

- Final: Don'**t** figh**t** a ca**t**, it bi**t** qui**t**e a lo**t** of mea**t**.

The velar plosives k and g

With the out-breath the soft palate rises and closes off the nasal pathway. The back of the tongue touches the velum or soft palate, stopping the air from escaping. There is a build-up of pressure followed by the tongue relaxing and the pressure is released.

Feel it first

Repeat these using the velar plosives:

Kkk ka, kkk ka, kkk ka
Ggg ga, ggg ga, ggg ga.

Practise it

The voiceless /k/

- Initial: **K**athy **k**indly **k**ept **c**amping **c**ostumes in the **c**ar.
- Medial: Po**k**ing and smo**k**ing the chi**ck**en.
- Final: Chic**k** pec**k** and pic**k** a ca**k**e.

The voiced /g/

- Initial: **G**andalf's **g**reat **g**ifts have **g**one to **G**hana.
- Medial: Hun**g**ry or**g**anic fi**g**ures re**g**ularly tri**gg**er the ja**g**uar.
- Final: Bi**g** ru**g** lo**g** tu**g** fo**g** mu**g** ago**g**.

F and v fricatives

The top teeth come into contact with bottom lip, teeth almost grabbing the bottom lip. The build-up of air pressure forces the air to rush through making a friction type sound.

Practise it

Voiceless /f/

- Initial: **F**ancy **f**ellows **f**ollowing **F**riday's **p**hilistines.
- Medial: Bu**ff**ers a**ff**ect a**f**ros.
- Final: Enou**gh** sta**ff**.

Voiced /v/

- Initial: **V**erily **v**ampires **v**alue **v**erse.

- Medial: Be**v**erage is tri**v**ial.
- Final: Wea**v**e a slee**v**e in a hi**v**e

Dental fricatives

The blade of the tongue comes into contact with the top teeth, because of this obstruction it forces the air to rush through on the outward breath (exhalation) making a sound as if there is friction.

Practise it

Voiceless /th/

- Initial: **Th**inkers **th**ought **th**eatre was **th**rough.
- Medial: A**th**letes and my**th**icals have a me**th**od.
- Final: Tee**th** unear**th** tru**th**.

Voiced /th/

- Initial: **Th**ose **th**at and **th**is **th**en **th**ere and over **th**ere.
- Medial: Ano**th**er sou**th**ern mo**th**er.
- Final: Brea**th**e and wri**th**e.

Alveolar fricatives

The obstruction is caused by the blade of the tongue coming into contact with the alveolar ridge. The pressure from your breath builds up and forces air to rush through making a friction sound.

Feel it first

Repeat these using the alveolar fricatives:

Sss, sss, sss
Zzz, zzz, zzz.

Practise it

Voiceless /s/

- Initial: **S**ip a **s**op and **s**auce the **s**andwich.
- Medial: As a bra**c**elet and par**c**el it in par**s**ley.
- Final: Ni**c**e voi**c**e ni**c**e voi**c**e ni**c**e voi**c**e.

Voiced /z/

- Initial: **Z**esty **z**oo and **z**ip it with **z**eal.
- Medial: Ha**z**y re**s**olution impo**s**es no**s**es she suppo**s**es.
- Final: He ha**s** crui**s**e and play**s** ja**zz**.

Nasals

The nasal sound is characterized by nasal resonance. The obstruction occurs so that no air escapes through the mouth and, with the soft palate lowered, is forced into the nasal pathway; the sound comes down through the nose.

Feel it first

Repeat these as nasals:

Mmm mmm mmm ma, mmm mmm mmm ma, mmm mmm mmm ma

Nnn nnn nnn na, nnn nnn nnn na, nnn nnn nnn na, nnn nnn nnn na.

Practise it

/m/ the bilabial nasal.

The two lips come together to form an obstruction, and the sound escapes through the nose.

- Initial: **M**any **m**en called **M**onty **m**ake **m**oney with **m**yrtle and **m**agnolias.

- Medial: Li**m**p with a la**m**p and co**mm**ute.
- Final: Ha**m** a thu**m**b and bea**m**.

/n/ the alveolar nasal.

The blade of the tongue comes into contact with the alveolar ridge closing off the air stream to the mouth and forcing the air through the nose.

- Initial: The **n**osy **kn**ight **kn**itted the **n**asty **n**ightgown.
- Medial: Ba**n**d arou**n**d a pic**n**ic.
- Final: Moa**n** and sa**n**e are not a pu**n** on la**n**e, ra**in** and go**n**e.

The velar nasal

During exhalation when on voice the back of the tongue comes into contact with the soft palate completely closing off air to the mouth and causing the air to come down through the nose. Medial and final positions only.

Practise it

/ng/ is an example to use.

- Medial: Si**ng**er is si**ng**le when si**ng**ing.
- Final: The you**ng** the to**ng**ue su**ng**.

Here are some extra sounds in the initial position:

- W as in **W**ant a **w**ig, **w**ear a **w**ig, **w**eave a **w**ig.
- L as in **L**ick a **l**olly, **l**ose a **l**olly, **l**eave a **l**olly
- Sh as in **sh**ady in the **sh**ed, **sh**owers **sh**ould **sh**uffle.
- Ch as in **ch**imes **ch**ime in **Ch**ina.
- Dj as in **G**eorge's **J**ourney was a **j**oke.
- Y as in **y**es **y**ou **u**sed **y**our **y**ummy **y**ear.

Consonant and vowel combos

Below is a list of words and sounds that build consonant combinations and vowel exploration. This helps warm up the voice, gives a stronger identity to sounds and yet the words are nonsense.

Feel it first

The vowel key and how they sound:

- OO as in spoon.
- OH = so.
- AW = saw.
- AH = star.
- AYE = say.
- EE = see.

The vowel sounds are added to the consonants below, and the consonant sound must be truly realized after each vowel combination at the end of each 'word', going down the alphabet.

OOB OHB ORB AHB AYB EEB
OOD OHD ORD AHD AYD EED
OOF OHF ORF AHF AYF EEF
OOG OHG ORG AHG AYG EEG
OOJ OHJ ORJ AHJ AYJ EEJ
OOK OHK ORK AHK AYK EEK
OOL OHL ORL AHL AYL EEL

OOM OHM ORM AHM AYM EEM
OON OHN ORN AHN AYN EEN
OOP OHP ORP AHP AYP EEP
OOS OHS ORS AHS AYS EES
OOT OHT ORT AHT AYT EET
OOV OHV ORV AHV AYV EEV
OOZ OHZ ORZ AHZ AYZ EEZ
OOTH OHTH ORTH AHTH AYTH EETH (voiced /th/)
OOTH OHTH ORTH AHTH AYTH EETH (voiceless /th/).

Understand it

These wonderful combinations of vowel and consonant allow a development of fully committed sounds; after all they are nonsense sounds, and yet by fully committing to nonsense sounds you create an energy with the articulators that when speaking 'real words', they too begin to feel more committed. The text has more juice, it feels bitten into and creates energy which carries at a distance, and very useful when working in an open space. The difference between the words *wha?* and *what?* in an open space such as Shakespeare's Globe theatre makes a big difference to what is heard.

Practise it

Now try the same vowel combination with the consonants at the beginning:

BOO BOH BOR BAH BAY BEE
DOO DOH DOR DAH DAY DEE
FOO FOH FOR FAR FAY FEE
GOO GOH GOR GAR GAY GEE
HOO HOH HOR HAR HAY HEE
JOO JOH JOR JAR JAY JEE
KOO KOH KOR KAR KAY KEE
LOO LOH LOR LAR LAY LEE

MOO MOH MOR MAR MAY MEE
NOO NOH NOR NAH NAY NEE
POO POH POR PAH PAY PEE
ROO ROH ROR RAH RAY REE
SOO SOH SOR SAH SAY SEE
TOO TOH TOR TAR TAY TEE
VOO VOH VOR VAR VAY VEE
WOO WOH WOR WAR WAY WEE
ZOO ZOH ZOR ZAR ZAY ZEE.

Next try the consonants either side of the vowels, such as:

BOOB, BOHB BORB BARB BAYB BEEB
DOOD DOHD DORD DARD DAYD DEED
FOOF FOHF FORF FARF FAYF FEEF.

Continue all the way through the alphabet using the same vowel sequence as above.

The combinations of consonants can begin to develop further by adding two consonants at the end of the sequence:

OOBD OHBD ORBD AHBD AYBD EEBD
OOPT OHPT ORPT AHPT AYPT EEPT
OOGD OHGD ORGD AHGD AYGD EEGD
OOKT OHKT ORKT AHKT AYKT EEKT
OOST OHST ORST AHST AYST EEST
OOZD OHZD ORZD ARZD AYZD EEZD.

These are tricky as both the g and the d or the k and t must be fully engaged to appreciate the energy of the consonants. This makes you very aware of your consonants and the muscularity required.

Now try a third consonant and see how that feels in your mouth and the muscularity that is required:

OOSKT OHSKT ORSKT AHSKT AYSKT EESKT.

Patter speak, rap and poetry

What is a patter song or patter speak? It could be considered similar to alliterated poetry or rap. The patter song is a common feature in musicals; it often has a light and rapid melody, using alliteration. This will often take the form of a long list or series of commands, and most commonly will involve tongue-twisters that test the singer's or speaker's ability to pronounce the lyrics clearly. Often the metre is raised further by increasing the tempo, sometimes as fast as 150 beats per minute (BPM). A semi-patter song is a toned-down version to that of a patter song, but the words become more important than the rapid delivery or melody.

Feel it first

Speak the following poem, 'Crazy Flower Shop', getting faster and faster whilst keeping the diction nice and clear.

Acers and Begonias, Cordylines and Foxgloves.
Geraniums and Grasses, Junipers and Jasmine.
Hibiscus and Hydrangeas, Ivies in the main.
Lupines like lollipops, even when it rains.
Mind your own business, Nandinas, nice and small,
Sunflowers and Wallflowers, crazy flower shop.

Understand it

The use of alliteration is a literary device that repeats a speech sound in a sequence of words that are close to each other, and typically uses consonants at the beginning of a word to give stress to its syllable. It also plays a very crucial role in poetry and literature, providing a wonderful vehicle when working with many musicals with diverse rhythms and pace.

In order to be proficient in this genre, it is essential to practise speaking very fast and often on a single note, or with as few notes as possible. This is particularly good for both speech and song. The famous operettas of Gilbert and Sullivan are prime examples, such as the patter song 'I am the Very Model of a Modern Major-General' from *The Pirates of Penzance* (1878); however there are patter songs that exist within more 'legit' songs in musical theatre such as 'I'm Getting Married Today' from the musical *Company* (1970) by Stephen Sondheim, and others such as 'The Speed Test' from *Thoroughly Modern Millie* (1967) by Dick Scanlan and Jeanine Tesori, or Kander and Ebb's 'Money' from *Cabaret* (1966).

Practise it

Try out being a modern major-general.

I am the very model of a modern Major-General,
I've information vegetable, animal, and mineral,
I know the kings of England, and I quote the fights historical
From Marathon to Waterloo, in order categorical;
I'm very well acquainted, too, with matters mathematical,
I understand equations, both the simple and quadratical,
About binomial theorem I'm teeming with a lot o' news,
With many cheerful facts about the square of the
   hypotenuse.

I'm very good at integral and differential calculus;
I know the scientific names of beings animalculous:

In short, in matters vegetable, animal, and mineral,
I am the very model of a modern Major-General.

I know our mythic history, King Arthur's and Sir Caradoc's;
I answer hard acrostics, I've a pretty taste for paradox,
I quote in elegiacs all the crimes of Heliogabalus,
In conics I can floor peculiarities parabolous;
I can tell undoubted Raphaels from Gerard Dows and
    Zoffanies,
I know the croaking chorus from *The Frogs* of Aristophanes!
Then I can hum a fugue of which I've heard the music's din
    afore,
And whistle all the airs from that infernal nonsense
    Pinafore.

Then I can write a washing bill in Babylonic cuneiform,
And tell you ev'ry detail of Caractacus's uniform:
In short, in matters vegetable, animal, and mineral,
I am the very model of a modern Major-General.

In fact, when I know what is meant by 'mamelon' and 'ravelin',
When I can tell at sight a Mauser rifle from a Javelin,
When such affairs as sorties and surprises I'm more wary at,
And when I know precisely what is meant by 'commissariat'
When I have learnt what progress has been made in
    modern gunnery,
When I know more of tactics than a novice in a nunnery
In short, when I've a smattering of elemental strategy
You'll say a better Major-General has never sat a gee.

For my military knowledge, though I'm plucky and adventury,
Has only been brought down to the beginning of the
    century;
But still, in matters vegetable, animal, and mineral,
I am the very model of a modern Major-General.

Rap

To rap means to strike, blow or hit and is used both as a verb and a noun, and it is used to describe rapid speech. Rap as a musical genre can be mistaken for singing, speaking and chanting, as contemporary beat poets rap, and singers rap. Rapping is distinct in that it is generally performed to a beat or tempo, often up to 160 BPM. The components of rapping can include fast-paced delivery, alliteration and rhyme. It can be delivered over a beat or without accompaniment. The most famous musicals that use rap are Lin-Manuel Miranda's *Hamilton* (2015) and *In the Heights* (2005), *Into the Woods* (1986) by Stephen Sondheim, and even *The Music Man* (1975) by Meredith Wilson and Frank Lacey. The mathematician and poet Harry Baker raps extremely well in his book of poems *The Sunshine Kid*.

Rapping is a form of poetry that is performed to a beat, with rhyme and rhythm playing an important part of quick speech and singing, and although rapping is more associated with hip-hop music, it can be used in forming a relationship between speech and song.

Feel it first

Try rapping this section of text below about hair. Start with 80 BPM to get familiar with the rhythm and the words, then build-up to 160 BPM which feels more natural to a rap beat.

Snip snip
Silly long hairstyle, silly billy hairstyle
Don't want to get a haircut, don't want to get it now
My momma says it's too long, my daddy says fine –
My sisters are complainin', it's longer than theirs –
Yet girlfriends like to touch it, running through their hands.
Snip snip

Silly long hairstyle, silly billy hairstyle
My homeboys say just keep it, they say it looks fine
My teacher he don't like it and want it like marines.
Buzz buzz
I'm gonna keep my hair long, don't care what you say.
My hair is like a curtain and acts like a screen,
My head is cool and on hot days, and warm when it
    freeze.
My buddies they all like it, my girlfriends say I'm cool,
My daddy says I'm like him and not some crazy fool.
Whoop whoop

Practise it

Try writing a rap yourself. Think of a simple topic and also the beats you want to work it at. Then explore with the beat what works; you may need to change the odd word here and there until it feels right. Some suggested topics are listed below:

Trees and flowers
Hot weather versus cold weather
Candy and other sweets
Skateboarding and rollerblading
Relationships.

Suggested rap artists or rap songs to consider:

Busta Rhymes
Karmin, 'Look at Me, I'm Making Paper'
Nova Rockafellar
Shellz, 'Turnt Up' remix
Legga. C, 'Who Got the Heater'
Mac Lethal, 'Look at Me Now I'm Making Pancakes'.

Tips for teachers

Using a simple beat, beginning quite slowly, with as few
notes as possible, is the best way to start when
improvizing with this style of teaching rapid speech. Using
a metronome (there are many you can download for free)
allows you to control the speed of delivery. Start off with
80 BPM (which is actually quite slow), and then increase
the BPM week by week until you feel the students can be
understood at the immensely faster pace. Encourage the
students to explore other poetry or even Shakespeare's
sonnets, by trying a combination of the 14 lines, where
some are rapped, some which are sung, and some which
are spoken. This will engage the students both in terms of
classical text, fast-paced delivery, speech and song. Further
work can be explored via the British hip-hop star and poet
Akala, who works on many of Shakespeare's texts
including working with the Hip-hop Shakespeare
Company. Perhaps try the third chorus speech from *Henry
V* in rap, speech and song.

> Thus with imagined wing our swift scene flies
> In motion of no less celerity
> Than that of thought. Suppose that you have seen
> The well-appointed King at Hampton pier
> Embark his royalty, and his brave fleet
> With silken streamers the young Phoebus fanning.
> Play with your fancies, and in them behold
> Upon the hempen tackle ship-boys climbing;
> Hear the shrill whistle which doth order give
> To sounds confused; behold the threaden sails,
> Borne with th' invisible and creeping wind,
> Draw the huge bottoms through the furrowed sea,
> Breasting the lofty surge.

Suggested texts

Here are some suitable texts for you to try:

Noel Coward, 'Mad Dogs and Englishmen'
Douglas Furber and L. Arthur Rose, music by Noel Gay, *Me and My Gal*: 'An English Gentleman'
Rupert Holmes, *The Mystery of Edwin Drood*: 'Both Sides of the Coin'
Gerard Manley Hopkins, 'Brothers'
Tom Leher, 'The Elements'
Kurt Weil and Ira Gershwin, *Lady in the Dark* contains Danny Kaye's famous list of Russian composers, 'Tchaikovsky'
Meredith Wilson, *The Music Man*: 'Ya Got Trouble' and 'Rock Island'

Further reading

Baker, H. (2014), *The Sunshine Kid*, Burning Eye.

Carey, D. and R. Carey Clark (2008), *Vocal Arts Workbook and DVD*, London: Methuen Drama.

Fisher, J. and G. Kayes (2016), *This is a Voice*, London: Wellcome Collection.

McCallion, M. (2010), *The Voice Book*, rev. edn, London: Routledge.

Parkin, K. (1962), *Ideal Voice and Speech Training*, New York: Samuel French.

Rodenburg, P. (1997), *The Actor Speaks*, London: Methuen Drama.

Turner, J. C. (2007), *Voice and Speech in the Theatre*, 6th edn, ed. Jane Boston, London: A & C Black.

6 Resonance

Keywords: resonance, placing, vibrations

To purr like a cat is to feel the power of unsaid thoughts.
CHINESE PROVERB

Introduction

What do we mean when we say 'I like that actor because he has strong chest resonance' or 'I like how she can throw her voice and she has so much warmth to her voice. Now how do I get that resonance?' We are often spellbound by the quality of tone, resonance and warmth that an actor utilizes within their spoken voice – sometimes more than the words being spoken.

In this final chapter the aim is to bring all the elements of the speaking voice together, using resonance as its vehicle, and so encourage the awareness of what resonance is, how to explore it, and how to develop it and keep it. There are exercises to increase vibrations, which also deliver power and pitch range, deepening the connection to all the previous voice work in earlier chapters. We will explore placing the sound for various accents and what an accent does for character development, and further develop resonance in social settings and other mediums.

How often have you been tempted by food and drink if you listen to advertisements on TV and radio? You can hear the tone and colour of the voice as it creates feelings that make us want to buy the product, such as the cake, the ice-cream, chocolate or drink, primarily because the voiceover has tempted us so much. Resonance brings a warmth and colour to the sound; I like to think of it as almost a 3-D image in sound. Without resonance a voice can sound quite thin, and the image I have for a thin voice, without much resonance, is a slice of processed cheese, thin and a little dull and flat. Instead, can you imagine your voice so full of resonance, colour and warmth that it sounds round like a giant bubble? That is the image I like to think of when a voice has fully formed resonance.

Feel it first

It is useful to record a few lines of text, either counting or reciting something, or even reading from a book. This helps you to place your sound where it is right now. Perhaps make a note of how your voice feels to you, how it sounds to you, as you record yourself with a sentence or two that you will speak again later.

- Stand in neutral, quietly hum with your jaw open and your lips gently closed so that you can feel vibrations on your lips, keeping the volume low. (If level 10 is the loudest then you want to start off around level 3 or 4.) Do this for about 1 minute.

- Now place one hand just below your throat area on the bone known as the clavicle; continue to hum trying to place the sound into this area.

  Can you feel the vibrations? What happens if you increase the volume to level 6 or higher?

- Now place your hand on the back of your neck and hum, trying to place the sound into your neck area, starting first on level 4 and increasing to level 6 or 7. Continue to check-in with your voice and body; check your jaw is open and lips are pursed gently closed.

- Now change the note that you are humming on, perhaps glide up and down the scale. Do this for about 1 minute.

  Can you feel the vibrations on the back of your neck cut out around the passagio (the break in your voice)?

Can you increase the vibrations if you change the notes?

What does it feel like if you change the volume level, does this make the vibrations stronger?

- Now place two fingers gently on either side of your nose, and begin to hum, starting off quietly, humming around level 3 or 4, then increase the volume to about level 6. Avoid pressing down too hard with your fingers as you still want to feel the vibrations on your fingers. Do this for about 1 minute.

- Now change the note you are humming on.

- Next hum into the back of your neck, continue on the same note. *Are the vibrations still as strong?* Perhaps now change the note and see if the vibrations become stronger. Do this for about 1 minute.

How does it feel? Is there a greater degree of vibrations when you change the note or increase the volume? What do you feel?

Can you feel the vibrations as the soundwaves move and bounce around your body?

- Now let us develop the sound further, begin by humming on any note, then allow the lower jaw to come away so that the mouth falls open and start to create the AH vowel sound.

- Repeat the hum and allow the jaw to fall open and the 'ah' sound to release on the breath.

- Create a sequence of mmm aaa, mmm aaaaa, sounds, moving from feeling the vibrations in the hum, then open the sound to the 'ah' sound, like the word 'mah'. Do this for about 1 minute.

- Now as you continue to build the hum, allow the jaw to relax and create the 'aye' sound, so that you are in a cycle of mmm aye, mmm aye, like the word 'may'. Do this for about 1 minute.

- Continue to hum and build a cycle of the 'mmm' with the 'ee' sound, like the word 'me'. Do this for about 1 minute.

- Next hum for a moment and release the cycle of sound on the 'mmm' with the 'or' sound, like the word 'more'. Do this for about 1 minute.

- Continue to enjoy the hum and then release the cycle of sound on the 'mmm' with the 'ooo' sound, much like the word 'moo', intone this sound. Do this for about 1 minute.

Can you hear it?

Now re-record your voice speaking the same text as you did at the beginning of this chapter. Then play back both your first recording and your second recording.

Has the quality of your voice changed? Is there a rounder, richer, quality to the resonance? How does your voice feel in your body? Is your head vibrating?

Can you see it?

Using a spectrogram, or the voice recording app on your iPhone, will give you an idea of how your voice vibrates at frequencies; it is a visual representation of the spectrum of frequencies and it allows you to 'see' the vibrations of your voice. Your phone recordings may give you the chance to 'see' your voice and the soundwaves you make. Perhaps play the recordings one after the other and notice if there is any difference in the sound waves made on the graph at the beginning of a voice session and at the end in terms of peaks and troughs. It may look like there is more movement across the graph.

Understand it

What is resonance? The short answer is the frequency of sounds that feel like vibrations which are created through primary and secondary chambers, amplified by the movement of the vocal folds sitting in the larynx. We are all individuals and our anatomy determines some of how we will sound, but thorough working on resonance means you are able to improve the quality of resonance through the changeable shape of your vocal tract, the pitch and your breath management. A good, fully resonant voice will come from a long, wide vocal tract as your body acts like an amplifier, and it is the shape of your larynx, throat and mouth that determines your individual sound. You find this most obviously when listening to an opera singer speak.

If you imagine seeing a live band you will feel the vibrations of the music, the bass and the treble booming out at different frequencies. Well, that is pretty much what your body does as it resonates.

Female and male resonance

How do we get resonance? Learning to access and activate primary and secondary resonating chambers is one way. Sending the sound forward sometimes known as forward placement is another way. Placing the sound in a particular place in your body is another means of accessing the resonance. This doesn't mean your voice actually comes from the top of the head or neck or chest, but it means you have the ability to feel the vibrations through the bony structures of your skull, ribs or hard palate.

There are differences in the male and female voices in regards to anatomy and its resonance. For example, in men testosterone matters! It affects the change and growth of vocal folds and the laryngeal cartilages as they can grow anywhere between 16 and 24 mm in length, and are also thicker than the females vocal folds. Males have a longer vocal tract and bigger vocal folds and there is a more noticeable growth in these areas around puberty, hence the 'voice breaking' and the larger 'Adam's apple' – the laryngeal prominence – which sits on top of the thyroid gland, affecting the sound in terms of frequency.

The female vocal folds will grow to around 17 mm over the course of her life. Again this will be a contributing factor which affects pitch.

Good examples of strong resonance in a male-speaking voice would be Bryn Terfel, Benedict Cumberbatch, Morgan Freeman and, in musicals, Michael Ball, Alfie Boe, Bertie Carvel, Hugh Jackman and Billy Porter. Good examples of strong resonance in female actors, especially in musical theatre, include Imelda Staunton, Jennifer Holliday, Kerry Ellis, Kristin Chenoweth, Patti Lupone, Ruthie Henshall and Maria Friedman.

Men who speak with a low vocal range or from a fundamental frequency of below middle C will invariably be a bass or baritone singer. That is not to say they cannot be trained to sing as a tenor, but the thickness of the folds will indicate what is more natural and easier for the male. The same can be said of the women, whose fundamental frequency is above middle C, and are more likely to be a soprano. Again, this is where the natural voice will sit; however, with training it is possible to utilize other parts of the vocal range, in speaking and singing.

The fundamental frequency is the rate at which the vocal folds open and close. A clear way to understand this is to see a thin fold mass as moving at a fast rate which will give you a higher note and a higher frequency, if you were measuring it on an oscilloscope (an instrument used to analyse and explain waveforms of electrical signals; oscilloscopes are often used to look at the vocal folds in order to determine potential voice related issues). The data collected measures the wave patterns, the shape, movement and quality of the folds. A thick fold mass will give you a lower note, because the frequency at which they move will be slower and the note produced will be lower.

Practise it

(Video)

Point the sound, slap the sound, and share the sound exercise. Do this for about 10 minutes.

- Begin by standing in the neutral plus (N+) position.
- Hum, keeping the volume low to medium, keeping the jaw nice and relaxed.
- Next release on an open mouth on an AH vowel, whilst simultaneously pointing to somewhere across the room, sending the sound to that specific point.
- Continue to do this but change the notes and where you're pointing.
- Continue the above with different vowel sounds.
- Next slap your chest with the palm of your hand, as you extend the sound from a hum to an imaginary audience member.
- Repeat the exercise again, hum on your centre note; this time slap your chest with both hands, sending your sound out into the wider world.
- Next hum some words of text.
- Hum a sound placing it in your nasal area.
- Hum a sound placing it in your chest area.
- Hum a sound placing it in your head area.
- Speak a line of text feeling your voice fully resonating.

Extending the resonance

Now we look at extending the sound of resonance; this exercise allows time for the resonance to sit within the body, creating energy whilst being focused and specific.

Work through the light sabre exercise. Do this for about 10 minutes.

- Check in with your posture of N+ with your jaw open and relaxed and your lips gently pursed together.

- Gently hum and treat the hum as an initial base line of where you are right now.

- Imagine that when you open your mouth a shaft of light emerges, much like the light sabre from the Stars Wars films. *What colour do you see your light?*

- Look at everyone in the room, or if you are alone, look at all the objects in your room, and allow your jaw to drop from the hum to a vowel sound, perhaps the AH sound to start with.

- The imaginary light that comes from your mouth can hit the object or another person in the room. (For sensitive purposes it would be more useful to use the light sabre for good rather than evil thoughts.) You are bathing that person in the lovely glow of your mouth light, it shines like a torch so bright. Imagine your light is also your voice, as you allow your voice to literally shine at another person or object, allowing that person to glow because of your light.

Does the colour of your light change? What texture is the light?

Tips for teachers

If you have time, split your group into two: it can be by gender, or by voice identified in bass, baritone, tenor, soprano and alto, or you could leave the choice up to the group. I have noticed that some voices carry further and can be more forceful, driving the overall sound in a particular direction, and therefore splitting the group allows more scope for experimentation. This allows the possibility for the voices to harmonize together, creating a unique quality of sound. The higher range grouping sound will have its own unique qualities. The lower range group can also play with their range and explore their potential further, extending the resonance but overall creating a sound that is a collective. Finally, bring the groups back together and have one group close their eyes and listen to the sound of the other group. Then repeat with the other group. *What do they notice about the voices they are listening to? What are the advantages and disadvantages of this exercise? What do the students think about gender- or classification-based exercises?*

Higher resonance or soprano, mezzo-soprano and contralto, using duologues

Placing the sound in the forehead, chest, oral and nasal area and back of the neck.

- Start by chewing and humming, placing the sound in the nasal area. Raise your eyebrows as you continue to hum and chew.

- Speak a prepared duologue, where the conversation happens between your forehead and your neck.

- Place your hand on the area that you are sending the sound to. You speak both parts, being as specific as you can in placing the resonance into the head and neck area.

- Repeat the same duologue, this time placing the sound between the nasal and chest areas. Place your hand on the areas you are sending the sound to.

- Finally create a dimension of sound between head, chest, neck and nasal as you further explore the areas of specified resonance within the duologue. Place your hand on the areas you are sending the sound to.

What do you notice about your voice and your resonance? Does your voice feel 3-D?

Lower resonance countertenor, tenor, baritone and bass, using duologues

Placing the sound in the abdomen, chest and upper and lower back.

- Stand in neutral and hum into your lower back, then send the sound to your upper back. Place your hand on the area you want to send the sound to.

- Use a duologue to explore the resonance between the upper and lower back, and occasionally slapping your chest as we did in the earlier exercise.

- Next use a hum to place the sound in the chest area and your abdomen, creating a dialogue of two different sounds – almost like two different voices.

- Using the same duologue, speak the two different roles placing the sound into the chest and the upper back. Place your hand on the area you are sending the sound to.

- Continue with the same duologue, being as specific as you can, sending the sound to the nasal and the lower back areas.

- Now play with the four areas of sound.

  What do you notice about your voice and your resonance?

- Continue with the same duologue, this time placing the sound into the nasal, upper back and lower back and chest areas, creating a dimension of sound around your whole body.

  Does your voice feel like a 3-D voice?

Further exploration for all soprano, mezzo-soprano, contralto and countertenor, tenor, baritone and bass voices

- Start by humming into all eight areas or spaces. The areas are as follows: forehead, oral, neck, nasal, chest, abdomen, upper back, lower back.

- Imagine waves of sound coming from each of the areas, and continue to be specific in placing the sound according to the area you are working on.

- Take two resonating spaces, one from the lower list and one from the higher list.

- Start to hum into these two areas, creating a sound dialogue between them.

What does it feel and sound like?

Tips for teachers

Often a good exercise to do is to split the groups into genders and work with one half at a time. This provides the freedom for the students to own and explore each group's vocal quality and then can be opened out to a greater choice, placing the sound in the body parts to gain optimum resonance and balance the tone. This is not an attempt to be gender-biased but to recognize the vocal qualities of each gender, and then to allow a deeper exploration into the areas we generally find comfortable and those we generally avoid. I have found it can be difficult to ask a young woman to play a deeper and fully resonating quality of an older woman without depressing the larynx. These exercises enable those students who sit in a comfortable place in their vocal range to work beyond their perceived range.

Accents for musicals

Does it matter if the singing is different from the speaking in a play or musical? Yes it does. Whilst the singing takes away some of the sounds associated with speech, it nevertheless is important to keep the accent of the character consistent throughout.

Feel it first

Begin speaking a few lines of text, perhaps a monologue, and set them in a generic place. Let's begin with France. Walk around the room imagining you are French. *How are you moving around the room? How does it feel to use your voice and body in this way?* Whilst to begin with the accents may be generalized, this is fine as you gain confidence in this way.

Speak the lines below, having a stab at some generalized accents; for example, Californian, German, Italian, upper-crust English, Irish (North or South).

> How are you?
> Not today, George, its Sunday.
> Sing out, you will be a star.
> It has been too long.
> Sandy, I love the colour of your hair.
> What a gal, what a guy.
> I want to be free.
> I am sad, I want to go home.

Tips for teachers

Here are some other ways to investigate accents and voice qualities.

- Working in pairs, one of the students becomes an alien from the planet Zigast, and makes up their own

---

language whilst the partner translates what is being said to the rest of the group.

- Working in pairs, one of your students becomes the voice of Sir David Attenborough, whilst the other becomes the animal he is describing.

Understand it

Accents are a way of associating with a social class, an area or a country. It is the unique way in which you will speak. Sometimes there are prejudices against certain sounds. All of the accents you explore in musical theatre tell you a great deal about character, place and time, country, parentage, social class and so on. It gives a rich tapestry that adds to the uniqueness of the character and should not be underestimated. It should not be an afterthought, but instead seen as part of the research when playing a role. Look at a map of where the character is from and the countries or counties that border it. This helps develop the character into a more three-dimensional one. It also requires great listening skills and observational skills.

Practise it

In pairs, explore a series of improvized scenarios playing the accents set out below:

Palm reader (Texan): customer (French)
Hairdresser (Liverpool): customer having hair done (posh English).
Shoe shop owner (New York): customer taking back shoes (Cockney)

Here is a short list of accents in British-based musicals:

Cockney = *Sweeney Todd* by Stephen Sondheim (1979); *Oliver* by Lionel Bart (1960); *Me and My Gal* by Noel Gay (1937)

Liverpool = *Blood Brothers* by Willy Russell (1983)

Sheffield = *Everybody's Talking about Jamie* by Tom McCrea (2017)

Northern Irish = *The Beautiful Game* by Andrew Lloyd Webber and Ben Elton (2008); *Once* by Glen Hansard and Marketa Irglova (2011)

Below is a short list of American-based musicals that all require unique accents:

New York = *Guys and Dolls* by Frank Loesser (1950); *Hello Dolly* by Jerry Herman (1964)

Oklahoma = *Oklahoma* by Richard Rodgers and Oscar Hammerstein (1943)

Texan = *Best Little Whore House in Texas* by Carol Hall and Larry L. King (1982)

Listed below are some accents which are written by American lyricists and composers:

German = *The Sound of Music,* Rodgers and Hammerstein (1959); *Cabaret* by Kander and Ebb (1966)

Mimicry and impersonations

Feel it first

This can be done in pairs or, if you are working alone, find someone you can observe; at this stage, make it someone you know very well and make sure in the first exercises that they are the same gender as you.

- Start by warming up the voice, using some of the exercises from Chapters 4 and 5.

- Watch the other person intently as they talk to you about a subject you choose in advance.

- Observe and repeat the exact things they do and say, trying to be as specific as you can.
- Observe and repeat the things they do with their mouth.
- Try to create their baseline note, and again listen and be specific.
- Copy a phrase they say over and over.
- Then copy what they do with their facial mask; again be specific.
- Can you copy what they do with their hand gestures?
- Do they stress words? Try and copy.
- Do they have any habits? Observe and copy.

If you take these habits and make them a little more extreme than they really are, this would be known as an *impression* rather than a true *impersonation*. Enjoy perfecting the habit, this will give you something to hang the overall impersonation on.

- Now think about someone in public life that you would like to imitate, someone that has already exaggerated mannerisms, phrases or vocal qualities that make them unique. This is what you should try and focus your efforts on. Perhaps download a clip from YouTube, and repeat over and over whilst watching them, in the exact timeframe.
- Now try to physicalize their facial movements, tics, idiosyncrasies, perhaps even their movements. Notice when they breathe, how they move, where they focus their eye movements, and where they place their sound.

  Is it a breathy sound? Is it a rich sound full of resonance? Or does it have sloppy and carefree articulation? Do they have a creak-like quality?
- Finally repeat the earlier exercise above to help you define the celebrity, actor or politician further. Perhaps it

becomes a party trick for you, or perhaps you can use it in a play or musical.

Understand it

Look at the great masters of impersonations and impressions from those in the UK such as Rory Bremner, Jon Culshaw, Alistair McGowan and Luke Kempner, to famous impersonations in TV and film that have been highly acclaimed, with the likes of Marc Pickering in the HBO series *Boardwalk Empire* who impersonates the Steve Buscemi character in his earlier years; Meryl Streep as Margaret Thatcher in *The Iron Lady*; Claire Foy as Queen Elizabeth in the series *The Crown*; Gary Oldman as Winston Churchill in *Darkest Hour*; and Michael Sheen as Tony Blair in *The Queen*. The mastery these incredible performers have in common is a wonderful gift for listening. They listen to and observe the performers they are imitating in order to recreate that sound to perfection. They learn how to place the sound and use the manner or shape of the mouth to recreate that sound. This is also true of accent work, but the art of impersonations will take things to the next level. American impersonators such as Jim Meskimen have created whole careers based on the ability to impersonate others.

Imitation is to truly listen, truly observe, then master to the point of performing it. Specificity and preciseness becomes the key and then exaggerating can bring you immense confidence in working on impressions, accents and character traits. You will see many actors who wish to display their abilities on many talk shows, both in the USA and the UK. This shows the level of command of the voice and facial mask, including the ability to almost look like the person they are mimicking. Understanding the uniqueness of the voice in all its placements of sounds, such as the nasal quality of one individual over the breathy quality of another, allows the actor to precisely place the sound in different areas of the vocal tract, the resonators, the breath and tune.

Practise it

- Observe an actor from a film or television clip (about 3–5 minutes' worth).

- Hum their speaking voice as you watch that clip over and over again.

- Use just the vowel sounds to create and perfect the correct pitch.

- Once you have got the words perfected, speak at the same time as the clip so that you perfect the rhythm and pace of the actor you wish to impersonate.

- Now take it a stage further by expressing any vocal or physical tics or idiosyncrasies that the speaker has, for example a slight lisp, or a curl of the lip.

- Continue to play back the clip for reassurance that you are not shifting or changing the sound in order to bring the sound closer to yourself, in order to keep the signature of the impression true.

- Perform it to someone and see if they can guess who you are.

Safe screaming, calling and shouting onstage

So you have been asked to scream and shout in a show such as *Carrie the Musical*, or to play the subway ghost in *Ghost the Musical*, or Grinpayne in the *Grinning Man*. All these roles ask for much shouting and screaming from the leads. The worry I receive which is common amongst young actors is that they will hurt their voice or, worse, lose their voice. First of all, don't panic. Many directors will ask this of you and you need to trust your vocal skills as they will want this repeated over and over again during rehearsals.

Feel it first

First, begin by marking your text where the shouting or screaming begins and ends. Look at what the character does before and after. This will give you time to set up the posture and also allow you to mark out the screaming on the page. Marking the text like this allows you to see where the breath patterns in shouting and speaking may be. Once you have established where these moments occur, it is possible to start working on the actuality of it. Secondly, from a health and safety point of view, it is possible to speak to a director to mark the 'shout' or 'scream' as if you were marking a song whilst working on a dance sequence. This gives you the opportunity to integrate more fully all the skills when in later rehearsals and full runs.

- Start by standing in neutral, then lean back to N+ as this will set up the physical pose. Always engage the image of the angel and her wings or the oranges under the armpits and squeeze. If you need to be reminded go back to Chapter 1 on the N+ posture (p. 15).

- Imagine you have won a leading role in a musical, having been through at least five recall auditions, and you have finally got it! Let out a whoop of joy, 'Whoo hoo'.

- Return to neutral posture, then lean into N+ and squeeze the imaginary oranges under the armpits and engage the back muscles.

- Let out a silent yelp, whilst still squeezing the oranges under the armpits.

- Move forward into neutral and gently siren up and down your scale, then swallow.

- Now lean back again for N+ and holler a shout and say 'hey'.

- Roll forward to neutral and gently siren up and down the scale.

- Now return to N+ and call out 'yeh hey', 'whoo hoo', 'oh no', 'oh my', 'oh no', 'oh wow', in succession.
- Roll forward to neutral and gently siren up and down your scale, then swallow.
- Now lean back for N+ and call a long vowel sound 'aye' as in 'hey'.
- Roll forward into neutral and swallow and siren up and down the scale.
- Then continue to lean back for N+ and aim for a scream, keeping the vocal tract open.
- Continue to stand in N+ and scream out the following words: 'NO', 'STOP', 'I CAN'T', LEAVE ME ALONE', 'I WILL SCREAM'.
- Now keeping in N+, let out a bloodcurdling scream.
- Now roll forward to neutral and gently siren up and down your scale, then swallow.

How do you feel? How does your voice feel?

Understand it

We often scream at a football match, the Olympics or other sporting events. It's natural and primitive and spontaneous, responding to external circumstances as mentioned above. The actor of course may have to scream several times a day in rehearsal and performance whilst being safe with the voice and breath. Marking the rehearsal and working on the posture is key in establishing a healthy scream night after night.

The physical posture of N+ allows you to feel your back and neck muscles, including your sternocleidomastoids, working to allow a frame to 'support' you. Your larynx will move up and down in a scream, moving through the vocal register in quick succession, and the open vowels at the beginning of the sequence allow you to practise screaming without the consonants stopping the airflow. Returning each time to a siren allows you to feel and hear your voice, and to check there are no vocal issues.

You do have to be careful about practising this at home. I had one ex-student who was practising for a role in a play over and over, as they were safe screaming. The neighbours thought he was being attacked and called the police, leading to a news item on BBC1 and a report in the London evening newspapers. So be mindful where you practise!

Practise it

Always start in the N+ position as it is a safe posture for this kind of work, and stops any potential vocal issues. Then return to neutral and begin the siren sequence exercise afterwards.

Here is a list of calls, shouts and screams to try:

Yeah, yeah, yeah
Oh my!
No way!
Help me please!
Ha, you lost!
Oi, give that back!
Come back here!
Stop him! Now!
Leave me alone!
Shut up! Shut up! Shut up!
Will you be quiet?
Ah me!
Oh you gods!

Using more heightened text can help you explore the use of the call, shout or scream to greater effect. The power of the words helps deliver the intention, the strength and communication of the words, releasing emotions that can be an outpouring of grief or pain. The effort to work in heightened text is the same as having to sing a song. Here is some text to explore the vocal power in shouting and perhaps screaming, where you think appropriate.

Coriolanus Act 1 Scene 4:

All the contagion of the south light on you,
You shames of Rome! You herd of – boils and plagues
Plaster you o'er, that you may be abhorr'd
Further than seen, and one infect another
Against the wind a mile! You souls of geese,
That bear the shapes of men, how have your run
From slaves that apes would beat! Pluto and hell!
All hurt behind, backs red, and faces pale
With flight and agued fear! Mend and charge home,
Or, by the fires of heaven, I'll leave the foe
And make my wars on you. Look to't. Come on;
If you'll stand fast, we'll beat them to their wives,
As they us to our trenches. Follow me!

Further text to work on from *Troilus and Cressida* Act 1 Scene 1:

Peace, you ungracious clamours! Peace, rude sounds!
Fools on both sides! Helen must needs be fair,
When with your blood you daily paint her thus.
I cannot fight upon this argument;
It is too starved a subject for my sword.
But Pandarus – O gods, how do you plague me!
I cannot come to Cressid but by Pandar;
And he's as tetchy to be woo'd to woo
As she is stubborn-chaste against all suit.
Tell me, Apollo, for thy Daphne's love,
What Cressid is, what Pandar, and what we?
Her bed is India; there she lies, a pearl:
Between our Ilium and where she resides,
Let it be called the wild and wondering flood,

Ourself the merchant, and this sailing Pandar
Our doubtful hope, our convoy and our bark.

Suggested texts

Here are some suitable texts from musicals and plays for you to try:

Carrie the Musical (1987), book Lawrence D. Cohen, lyrics Dean Pitchford, music Michael Gore
Lopa De Vega (1631), *Punishment without Revenge*
Ghost the Musical (2011), 'You gotta focus', book and lyrics Bruce Joel Rubin, Dave Stewart and Glen Ballard
David Mamet (1984), *Glengarry Glen Ross*
Thomas Middleton (1606), *The Revenger's Tragedy*
Arthur Miller (1947), *All My Sons*
The Grinning Man (2016), book Carl Grose, music Tim Phillips and Marc Teitler
Sophocles (*c.* 429 BCE), *King Oedipus,* translated by E. F. Watling

Further reading

Chapman, J. L. (2006), *Singing: A Holistic Approach to Classical Voice*, Oxford: Plural Publishing.
Chekhov, M. (2002), *To The Actor*, London: Routledge.
Cook, O. (2008), *Singing with Your Own Voice*, London: Nick Hern Books.
Cook, R. (2012), *Voice and the Young Actor*, London: Methuen.
Fisher, J. and G. Kayes (2016), *This is a Voice*, London: Wellcome Collection.
Hampton, M. and B. Acker (1997), *The Vocal Vision*, Illinois: Applause.
Houseman, B. (2002), *Finding Your Voice*, London: Nick Hern Books.
Shakespeare, William (2010), *The Complete Works of Shakespeare*, London: Arden.
Shewell, C. (2009), *Voice Work: Art and Science in Changing Voices*, Wiley and Blackwell.

Appendix 1: Sample Curriculum

The voice curriculum set out is merely an indication of how you can incorporate the workbook into your classes. These have been designed with semesters in mind, of one class for 2 hours per week. This can easily be adapted into terms and shorter or longer duration, depending on your institution. The workbook follows a pattern that is easy to adopt; therefore, I wouldn't start a voice class in resonance or articulation, but have designed the book to place the exercises in an order I think works best for the musical theatre student.

Semester 1: Foundations

Week 1. Warm-up in Chapter 1 followed by the full neutral plus (N+) engagement from the feet upwards, then the t'ai chi inspired breath and movement sequence.

Week 2. Warm-up in Chapter 1 followed by the full (N+) from the feet upwards then moving into breath with partners in Chapter 2.

Week 3. N+ from the feet upwards in Chapter 1, followed by Chapter 2 breath in t'ai chi sequence, ribs breathing in pairs, and hip openers wind pose. Rock and roll with vowels in Chapter 3, then into articulation in Chapter 5, lip gym, jaw spa, tongue-tastic.

Week 4. Continue as above followed by Chapter 6: Resonance and Chapter 4: Pitch and Tune.

Week 5. Continue as above followed by rock and roll with vowels Chapter 3: Building the Voice and Chapter 6: Resonance.

Week 6. Revisit Chapter 1, N+, followed by Chapter 3, *The self, At arm's length* and *To the world*, sending the sound, followed by Chapter 5, introducing the principles of the bone prop (fruit and veg).

Week 7. Most universities would have a reading week placed here, but it is a chance to ask the students to make up a 20-minute warm-up incorporating all they have learnt so far.

Week 8. Feet and hips, in Chapter 1, and revisit the t'ai chi breath and movement sequence followed by a long session on curling and uncurling the spine, then Chapter 3: Building the Voice. Introduce further bone prop work from Chapter 5, followed by samples of text.

Week 9. Begin this session with Chapter 3 and archetypes, followed by the exercises in Chapter 4: Pitch and Tune, and end the session with suggested texts.

Week 10. Start this session with some exercises from Chapter 3, intoning, Chapter 4: Pitch and Tune, then Chapter 5, lip gym, jaw spa, tongue-tastic and suggested texts.

Week 11. Begin this session with N+ feet upwards, then to Chapter 2, t'ai chi and breath, followed by Chapter 6: Resonance, with exercises and some suggested texts.

Week 12. Review samples of each chapter and ask the students to formulate their own warm-up for the following week to include all aspects of the book: posture, breath, building the voice, pitch and tune, articulation and resonance. This should be a 30-minute voice workout, which you will see the following week.

Week 13. Split the group into four. Each small group gets up for 30 minutes in their own small area of the studio where you are able to watch them create their own vocal workout, which should include all that you set out. They can have their phones on timer of 30 minutes and their notes. The other three groups watch the students and learn from them. Each group takes a turn. You can then observe how each student works through their version of the work; you could take notes and feedback in the following session.

Week 14. Review the semester's work, giving feedback notes on the previous week's voice workout and perhaps review what exercises were misunderstood, or common mistakes, or even the order the students placed the exercises in.

Semester 2: Advanced

In this semester it is good to review the work, taking more time in each exercise to fully develop a deeper connection to the voice/body/breath work.

Week 1. Back to basics with warm-up from Chapter 1 and N+, including the sequence for curling and uncurling the spine, then Chapter 5, lip gym, jaw spa, bone prop and the suggested text.

Week 2. Warm-up and t'ai chi inspired voice workout (Chapters 1 and 2) followed by intoning, Chapter 3.

Week 3. T'ai chi warm-up, Chapter 2, followed by Chapter 4, high and low pitch words and sentences. Chapter 5, the 3-minute challenge.

Week 4. N+ feet first, Chapter 1, followed by resonance and then chants in Chapter 6.

Week 5. T'ai chi humming sequence, Chapter 2, followed by stamina work and skipping.

Week 6. Review the work before the Easter Break.

Week 7. Easter.

Week 8. Back to basics after the break: Chapter 1, warm-up, then t'ai chi and stamina, Chapter 2, intoning, Chapter 3, calling and safe screaming and shouting, Chapter 6, followed by the suggested texts.

Week 9. As above, adding intoning, Chapter 3, and Chapter 4, chants. Class on Chapter 6: Resonance, followed by suggested texts.

Week 10. As above for warm-up, then adding patter speak, Chapter 5.

Week 11. As above, adding mimicry and accents in musicals, followed by suggested texts.

Week 12. As above, adding intoning and chanting, rap or patter speak from Chapter 5, then some suggested texts.

Week 13. Each student devises a warm-up that is for a meta-musical such *as Kiss Me Kate.*

Week 14. Review the year's work in a practical session ready for the following year.

Appendix 2: Bibliography and Resources

Bain, K. (2015), *The Principles of Movement*, London: Oberon Books.

Bainbridge, C. B. (1994), *Sensing Feeling and Action*, North Atlantic Books.

Baker, H. (2014), *The Sunshine Kid*, Burning Eye.

BBC (2004), *The Nation's Favourite Poems*, London: BBC Worldwide Ltd.

Berry, C. (2000), *Voice and the Actor*, London: Virgin.

Bloom, K. and R. Shreeves (1998), *Moves*, London: Routledge.

Boston, J. and R. Cook (2009), *Breath in Action*, London: Jessica Kingsley Publishers.

Brizendine, L. (2007), *The Female Brain*, New York: Bantam Books.

Bruford, R. (1950), *Speech and Drama*, London: Methuen.

Bunch, M. (1997), *Dynamics of the Singing Voice*, 4th edn, New York: Springer.

Carey, D. and R. Carey Clark (2008), *Vocal Arts Workbook and DVD*, London: Methuen.

Carey, D. and R. Carey Clark (2010), *The Verbal Arts Workbook*, London: Methuen.

Chapman, J. L. (2006), *Singing: A Holistic Approach to Classical Voice*, Oxford: Plural Publishing.

Chekhov, M. (2002), *To The Actor*, London: Routledge.

Cook, O. (2008), *Singing with Your Own Voice*, London: Nick Hern Books.

Cook, R. (2012), *Voice and the Young Actor*, London: Methuen.

Duffy, C. A. (2009), *New Collected Poems for Children*, London: Faber and Faber.

Estill, J. (1992), 'Basic figures and exercise manual'. From *A User's Guide to Voice Quality*, Pittsburgh, PA: Estill voice training systems.

Everett, W. A. and P. R. Laird (2002), *The Cambridge Companion to the Musical*, Cambridge: Cambridge University Press.

Fisher, J. and G. Kayes (2016), *This is a Voice*, London: Wellcome Collection.

Franklin, E. (2004), *Conditioning for Dance*, Leeds: Human Kinetics.

Garfield Davies, D. and A. F. Jahn (1999), *Care of the Professional Voice*, Oxford: Butterworth Heinemann.

Gutekunst, C. and J. Gillett (2014), *Voice into Acting*, London: Bloomsbury.

Hampton, M. and B. Acker (1997), *The Vocal Vision*, Illinois: Applause.

Hopkins, G. M. (2002), *The Major Works*, Oxford: Oxford World Classics.

Houseman, B. (2002), *Finding Your Voice*, London: Nick Hern Books.

Kayes, G. (2004), *Singing and the Actor*, 2nd edn, London: A & C Black.

Larkin, C. (1999), *The Virgin Encyclopedia of Stage & Film*, London: Virgin Books.

Leborgne, W. and M. Daniels Rosenberg (2014), *The Vocal Athlete*, Oxford: Plural Publishing.

Lessac, A. (1967), *The Use and Training of the Human Voice*, 2nd edn, New York: McGraw-Hill.

Linklater, K. (1996), *Freeing the Natural Voice*, Drama Publishers.

Long, R. (2008), *The Key Poses of Yoga*, Baldwinsville, NY: Bandha Yoga Publication.

McCallion, M. (2010), *The Voice Book*, rev edn, London: Routledge.

McCallion, M. (2012), *Voice Power*, Graz, Austria: Mouritz Publishing.

Meir, P. (2011), *Accents and Dialects for Stage and Screen*, Lawrence, KA: Paul Meir Dialect Services.

Melton, J. with K. Tom (2012), *One Voice*, 2nd edn, Illinois: Waveland Press.

Newlove, J. (1993), *Laban for Actors and Dancers*, London: Nick Hern Books.

Nicholls, C. (2008), *Body, Breath and Being: A New Guide to the Alexander Technique*, Hove: D and B Publishers.

Parkin, K. (1962), *Ideal Voice and Speech Training*, New York: Samuel French.

Robinson, K. (2001), *Out of Our Minds: Learning to Be Creative*, Mankato, MI: Capstone.

Robison, K. (2000), *The Actor Sings*, Portsmouth: Heinemann.

Rodenburg, P. (1992), *The Right to Speak*, London: Methuen Drama.

Rodenburg, P. (1994), *The Need for Words*, London: Methuen Drama.

Rodenburg, P. (1997), *The Actor Speaks*, London: Methuen Drama.

Rodgers, J., ed. (2002), *The Complete Voice and Speech Workout*, Montclair, NJ: Applause.

Rodgers, J. and F. Armstrong (2009), *Acting and singing with archetypes*, Montclair, NJ: Limelight Editions.

Shakespeare, William (1999), *The Sonnets and a Lover's Complaint*, London: Penguin Classics.

Shakespeare, William (2010), *The Complete Works of Shakespeare*, London: Arden.

Shewell, C. (2009), *Voice Work: Art and Science in Changing Voices*, Chichester: Wiley and Blackwell.

Spivey, N. and M. Saunders-Barton (2018), *Cross-Training in the Voice Studio*, San Diego, CA: Plural Publishing.

Stark, J. (2008), *Bel Canto: A History of Vocal Pedagogy*, University of Toronto Press.

Turner, J. C. (2007), *Voice and Speech in the Theatre*, 6th edn, ed. Jane Boston, London: A & C Black.

Recommended websites and organizations

http://voicecare.org.uk
https://voiceworkshop.co.uk
https://www.britishvoiceassociation.org.uk
https://www.themorrisonboneprop.com
https://nats.org
https://www.vasta.org

Video resources

All videos can be found at: https://vimeo.com/channels/1445241

Chapter 1: https://vimeo.com/323436413
Chapter 2: https://vimeo.com/323436988
Chapter 3: https://vimeo.com/323437119
Chapter 4: https://vimeo.com/323436056
Chapter 5: https://vimeo.com/323436169
Chapter 6: https://vimeo.com/323436307

Index

abdominal muscles 29, 56, 73
accents for musicals 166–70
accessing the breath 47–53
Alexander Technique 11–13
alignment 11–41
animals 86–8
archetypes 86–8
articulation 125–53
articulators 125–6, 145

banana shape 28, 30
bone prop 135–8
breath 43–76
breathy onset 101
build the voice 77–104

calling 91, 96, 171, 180
cat pose 26–31
chants 95, 119–22
chest resonance 155
choral 96, 119
consonants 46, 78, 125–53
core strength 26, 30, 43, 71–4
cow pose 25–31
curling and uncurling the spine
        30–1

dance
    and breath 43–76
    and movement 43–7,
        66–8
    and posture 9–40
diaphragm 43–76

exhalation 21, 22–8, 30, 43–76
external intercostal muscles
        49–50
extrinsic muscles 132–3

feet 10, 12–19

glottal 100–2
glottis 51
gym breath 63–5

happy baby pose 21–8
high pitch words 110–13
Hindi
    chant 119
    squat pose 21
hips 21, 25, 27–49

impersonations 168–70
inhalation 47–74
internal intercostal muscles 28, 39,
        52, 115
intoning 45, 77–104, 120
intrinsic muscles 132–3

jaw 23–4, 34–6, 125–53

knees 20–2

Laban, Rudolf 66–8
larynx 34, 99, 102, 109–73
lips 23, 89–117, 125–62
low pitch words 111–12

mimicry and impersonations 168–70
movement 43–73
musical theatre performer (MTP) 2, 3, 9

nasal resonance 142
neck 10–12, 32–40
neutral 9–79
    minus 9–79
    plus 9–79

oblique muscles 28, 56, 73

patter
    song 147–8
    speak 147–8
phonation 50–6
pitch and tune 105–23
place the sound 82, 94–5, 155–9, 163–5
poetry 147–52
posture 9–42, 72–80, 171–8
prana breathing 59–60

rap 107, 147, 150–2
relaxation 23, 71, 72, 77
resonance 155–75
ribs 28, 32–8, 47, 48–64

safe screaming 171–4

shoulders 11–15, 25–8, 32–79
shouting 78, 171–5
sirening 71, 90, 108, 115, 172–4
soft palate 89, 90, 108, 126, 139
sphynx pose 29–31
spine 11–15, 21–58, 71–3, 92–131
stamina 44–7, 65
supine 26–8, 54–72
support, breath 9–43, 73, 74, 115

table pose 25, 26, 30, 31
t'ai chi 44–7
tension
    emotional 23, 34
    hips 23
    jaw 18, 129–30
tongue 23, 34, 35, 108–18, 125–53
top line 32, 37, 72, 79
transverse muscles 57, 73

vertebrae 10, 12, 131
vocal folds 50–1, 69, 70, 100–60
vowel modification 126–70
vowels 77–103, 126–75

wind pose 55, 56

yoga 15, 21, 23, 55